Waltzing
WITH
WOLVERINES

FINDING CONNECTION AND COOPERATION
WITH TROUBLED TEENS

MARK ANDREAS

Published by Wovenwords Press
WovenwordsPress.com
Boulder, CO USA

WOVENWORDS PRESS

Cover illustration by Mark Andreas
Cover design by Brendon Eisenbart

Paperback book ISBN: 978-0-9968020-2-4
Kindle e-book ISBN: 978-0-9968020-0-0
ePub e-book ISBN: 978-0-9968020-1-7

Disclaimer:

As with any book, readers are advised to use their own best judgment with regards to using any specific information or approaches provided in this book. The suggestions and ideas shared in these pages are based on my experience, and may or may not be applicable to your specific situation. By reading this book, you agree that you are responsible for any results of your decisions and actions relating to your use of any information presented in this book.

Names appearing in this book have been changed to protect the privacy of the individual, except where I've been given express permission to use a given name.

Praise for Waltzing with Wolverines

"In 'Waltzing with Wolverines,' Andreas redefines how to build re-lationship and trust with so-called 'troubled' youth. In these pages, you'll find a treasure trove of teaching and leadership stories, tools, and techniques. But this book is about much more than a list of be-havior management strategies— it's a clarion call to re-envision our relationship with our young people by creating relationships that are simultaneously more empowering and more effective for instructors and students alike. This is a must read for anyone working in the fields of wilderness therapy and outdoor education."

—**Jay Roberts**, Ph.D.,
Associate Professor of Education, Earlham College

"This book is a wonderful guide, not only for parents of 'troubled' or 'resistant' kids, but for every parent. If Mark had given only bullet points, like so many other books do, I'd have read and forgotten them by now. Instead, through the memorable stories Mark tells, the lessons are still clear in my mind. I wish I could have read this wise book when our children were younger, but I'll buy it for them now before they make the same mistakes with our precious grandchildren."

—**Ben Leichtling**, Ph.D.
Author of *How to stop bullies in their tracks* and
Bullies Below the Radar.

"Waltzing with Wolverines is a remarkable piece of work. This is a book of practical, nuts-and-bolts wisdom about working with youth on the edge. Anyone who works with young people will find useful ideas and inspiration in these pages."

—**Mark Gerzon**,
author of *Leading through Conflict*
(Harvard Business School Press)

"If you are a parent, you need to commit the principles and techniques expressed in this book to your heart and mind so that you can remain sane during adolescence. If your child is already a teenager this book will become your and your child's best friend. Using the techniques expressed so eloquently by the author allows you not only to reconcile problems expressed *by your children, your spouse, your colleagues but also to reconcile the more frustrating and problematic* non-expressed *problems, all in a non-confronting manner. This book should be a mainstay of communication programs."*
—**Melissa J. Roth** CHt., Ph.D.

"Mark doesn't just discuss theories and philosophies of becoming a master facilitator for 'at risk' youth, he models how it works in almost any possible scenario with brilliance, patience and true genius! If you want to become a master leader with teens in any venue, then this book is your bible for how to do it with great humanness, compassion, humor and brilliance."
—**Kimberly Kassner,**
author of, *You're a Genius—And I Can Prove It!* and
Founder of EmpowerMind

Dedication

To the "troubled" "at risk" youth out there; having
parents can be a risky and troubling business.
This book is not written for you, but if you do read it
I hope you come away with a bag of tricks to play on
authority figures who won't listen to you or respect you
or engage in true relationship. Who knows,
maybe you'll even be able to teach them how to
do it, though it's not your job.

Contents

Self Care

More About Having Fun

More About Communication

More About Power Dynamics

SECTION III: Further Tales

Chapter Four

Chapter Five

Chapter Six

Chapter Seven

Preface

The tales and tools enclosed in these pages come from my experience working as a trip leader for a wilderness therapy program for "at risk" youth called the Monarch Center for Family Healing, based in the Colorado Rocky Mountains.

If you are a leader or counselor of "at risk" or "troubled" youth, then I am writing directly to you. However, if you are a teacher or parent (or anyone with a teen in your life), this book is equally for you. Whether your students or children are troubled or not, the principles demonstrated in these stories work the same. They are tried and true practical ways to have more fun, effective, and enjoyable relationships with the youth in your life.

In "SECTION I: Tales," I begin in the introduction by showing you why I modified one of the guiding principles that I was taught about working with teens, and how I found the key that allowed me to be comfortable in virtually every moment that I led, whether I was being threatened, cussed out, disobeyed, lied to, called "fish face" during an eight-hour van ride, or having cigarette smoke blown defiantly in my face. Following the introduction, the three chapters in this section give you a sampler of the marvelous chaos of our work environment and the boundless "creativity" of the kids. Each chapter is a story of an entire expedition that I led. You'll join in on my first expedition, which was a gentle introduction to this kind of work, another where everything went wrong, and a third that went very well. These chapters will give you a sense of how this program operated over an entire shift—the larger context in which I was working. Because we learn best through experience, having this broader view in your mind will help you understand how I worked with these kids, and make it easier for you to translate the important principles to your unique situation, whether that is leading a group, teaching a class, or relating to the teens in your life.

The entries in "SECTION II: Tools" are organized by specific subjects so you can easily scan through and find a method that is relevant to you. Each entry includes specific examples of how I used these tools in practice, so you can see when and where I used them, and how they worked for me.

The four chapters in "SECTION III: Further Tales" share additional stories from my experiences at Monarch, including two stories of how I dealt with angry teenage boys who completely defied me. Another chapter chronicles the time Monarch was hosted on the German Reality TV show "*Teenager* Außer Kontrolle" (Teenagers out of Control). The closing chapter in this section is an in-depth example of how I worked with a teen's family issues before he boarded a plane to fly back to rejoin his family.

At this point you may be wondering, "What exactly does it mean to be a trip leader (aka field instructor) for a wilderness therapy program for 'at risk' youth?"

"Field instructor" means I was in charge of leading backpacking trips for groups of 8-12 kids, ages ranging from 12-18, who did not want to be there. My office was the backcountry—the Rocky Mountains, and the deserts of Utah, Arizona, and New Mexico. My hours were 24/7 for three weeks in a row. (If everything went well, I'd get one night off.) At the most basic level my job was to keep the kids safe out in the elements for extended periods of time beyond the reach of cell-phones, from sub-zero blizzards in the mountains to triple-digit heat waves in the dessert. But as you'll soon find out, this is only the most basic definition of "field instructor."

"At risk," means teens who are alive, and their parents are worried. The kids were sent to us for many reasons—drugs, sex, anger, lying, breaking the law, gambling, stealing, running away, or sometimes just having neurotic parents. Parents had as many reasons for sending their kids as their kids had for not wanting to come. But basically, parents would send their teens to us when two things happened: their relationship with their son or daughter had deteriorated to a level where they no longer had any meaningful influence with them, *and* they felt their child was in some kind of danger, whether physical, psychological, or moral.

"Wilderness therapy," is fairly self-descriptive, as most of the therapy was unofficial and took place in the wilderness conducted by non-therapists (myself and the other field instructors). The kids were assigned official therapists and took part in family and group therapy sessions at the beginning of each 3-week expedition, and again half way through each expedition. I believe they received more therapy, and of higher quality, than almost any other program. But the fact remains that the kids were in official therapy only a very small fraction of the time they spent in our program. The rest of the time was spent with me, my co-instructor, and the great outdoors. Though "field instructor" doesn't have "therapist" anywhere in the title, we were the ones with the kids every moment of every day, including during their official therapy sessions. This meant that we had far more opportunities to do therapy than the therapists did, and all while teaching the kids how to live comfortably in the backcountry without getting eaten by mountain lions (or each other).

The final role of the field instructor is that we were also their surrogate parents. 24/7, we were their models for how to form healthy relationships. The kids watched us constantly, and usually let us know immediately when we screwed up. So we had to walk the talk. Faking it is not an option for three weeks straight.

The job of field instructor was a challenging role where average length of employment was measured in months, and many new to the job lasted only weeks. I worked at Monarch for more than two years as a field instructor—the longest that anyone stayed on in that role. This gave me a wealth of learning experiences regarding human behavior, positive leadership, and relationships. Each expedition brought something new and crazy to make me laugh or cry (or both) and keep me on my toes. There was rarely a dull moment.

What the kids got from the program is for them to say, but they definitely gave me a lot, and I thank them for that. Now I am passing it on in the following stories and learnings—the tales and the tools.

SECTION I: Tales

Introduction

The Key to it All

After just over two years as a field instructor, I walked into my boss' office to tell him I'd finally decided to move on to the next phase of my career. I don't know what I expected, but Nick's response surprised me: "I didn't think you'd last beyond your first expedition," the ex Army Ranger exclaimed, shaking my hand with a firm grasp despite missing nearly all of four fingers on his right hand. Then he hugged me.

"You didn't think I'd last beyond my first expedition?" I asked, taken aback. I admired and respected Nick not only for the way he seamlessly carried out his difficult job of hiring and overseeing field instructors (a responsibility I was glad to never have), but also for his wisdom in working and speaking directly with the kids in our program.

"When I first met you I thought the kids would eat you up," Nick said. "You seemed so kind and innocent."

Memories from expedition after expedition flooded through me, reminding me why so many field instructors *didn't* last. There was the time Toby drank his own pee and pooped in his hands, chasing the other kids around camp with the weapon of mass disruption, then dropping his bio-terrorism in favor of threatening to stab me with his tent stakes. There was Roger, who snuck in a bottle of Advil and took enough that he started hallucinating, frantically searching through his tent for a non-existent necklace that he eventually "found" but understandably had trouble putting on. There was the expedition when Tom and Ken stole my Subaru key and managed to use it to start the Monarch pick-up truck in the middle of the night, escaping to a nearby town where they robbed a ski shop, outfitting themselves with Billabong clothing before driving the wrong way down a one-way street only to discover a police car coming the other direction. Dawn ran away one night and hitch-hiked all the way to Kentucky. When I took Jordan to get a physical he lied to the doctor, saying he wanted to kill himself, so the hospital refused to give him back to me. On a service project in New Orleans three kids ran off at night and I chased them from bar to bar in the Monarch van (complete with butterfly logo and "Family Healing" painted on the side). And on our drive to New Mexico, Adrian had a temper tantrum and shattered the front windshield of the car.

Even at the very end of my time at Monarch, I never knew what strange adventure awaited. There were the girls who cheeked their meds, crushed them up, and did lines off the office toilet seat. Another group managed to find not only marijuana as we hiked through the Loveland ski area one summer, but also a pipe to smoke it in. Nicholas refused to be a part of Monarch and started walking away down a dirt road that went for miles through the desert (I followed after him in the van, where I could listen to music). Mik pretended to strangle himself with pea cord from his tent. Percy punched a tree and sprained his hand. Abe smuggled in a condom and flashed it to one of the girls (hopefully he's thought up better pick-up lines since). Four kids teamed up in the creative effort of growing mold on their old orange peels so they could use it to get high. And there was Ben, who went limp like a rag doll, refusing to move or speak at all, but he was considerate enough not to put up resistance when we needed to move him.

These experiences profoundly transformed my understanding of how to work with youth, teaching me vital lessons that I want to share with you, so you can be as impactful as possible with the kids in your life. Of course as I stood there in Nick's office, I didn't know that I'd be writing this book. At the time I simply gained a new appreciation for everything I'd learned along the way that helped me not only keep my job, but thrive in it. And of all the crucial tricks and tools that I learned, there was one important lesson that I'll never forget, because it gave me the key to it all, unlocking my ability to flourish where Nick originally thought I would fail.

It happened when I got into a confrontation with a student while I was leading my second expedition. The confrontation wasn't life threatening, nor was the conflict itself particularly noteworthy. But the interaction forced me to re-think my behavior and discover the confidence to easily face and out-pace much more difficult conflicts throughout the expeditions to come. What I learned—and soon confirmed through countless other experiences—became the baseline for everything I did with the kids, leading me to modify Monarch's most fundamental principle of teen leadership to fit my new reality.

The story begins the way many confrontations begin, with something very trivial that suddenly gets blown way out of proportion. It was the beginning of our backpacking expedition, and we had made camp on the side of a hill in a clearing with scattered pine and aspen. I told the students it was time to write their daily reflection paper, which they began to do, all except Jill. She refused.

"Jill, it's part of the assignment for being out here."

"I don't care."

Uh-oh, I thought, *this kid isn't doing what I tell her to do! I have to assert control...* "Alright Jill, you can have your dinner as soon as you finish." *Ha, that should do it, who wants to go hungry?*

"OK, I just won't eat."

The little brat! That was when I got an anxious feeling in my gut. *If I don't assert control now the whole group will realize their new leader is a pushover. It'll be mutiny! Here's my first power control battle,* I realized. Monarch's most fundamental principle, which they taught to all their field instructors, was, "Never get into a power control battle, but if you do get into a power control battle, win it." I had failed the first task of not getting in it, so I resolved to do whatever it took to win the battle.

"If you don't do the assignment, I'll take away one of your family overnights," I told Jill, playing my trump card. After each expedition, any kid that had been good would earn several nights to leave the field and be with their families who had travelled to Georgetown to participate in family therapy before the next expedition. Though most of the kids were in this program because of trouble with their families, they almost invariably preferred to spend time with their families rather than stay camping in the elements. Family overnights meant access to hot showers, restaurant food, candy, music, movies, technology, and all kinds of things the kids valued highly but didn't get out in the wilderness. Things had to be pretty bad with their families to forgo all of these benefits. During my two years at Monarch I can remember only one kid who opted to stay in the field rather than spend time with his family. To almost every student at Monarch, family overnights were valued higher than anything else.

"Fine, take away my overnight," Jill said angrily.

Gulp. What now? "If you don't do your assignment, I'm taking away *all* your family overnights," I proclaimed, and I turned around and retreated to my tent, having exhausted my largest round of ammunition.

I felt awful. I was pretty much praying for her to finish the stupid assignment so I wouldn't have to take away all her family overnights. I really didn't want to do that to her. I had blown things completely out of proportion, and all because I'd felt trapped into having to assert my authority. I'd been told that if I got into a power control battle, I should win it, and as it turns out, that's what I did. Jill ended up doing the assignment, and I let her keep her overnights, but still it felt all wrong. What was the point of threatening a kid to obey you? That isn't therapy, it's awful.

That got me thinking a lot during my off-shift, and when I came in for my next three-week expedition leading a new group of eight male teens, the first thing my boss said got me thinking even more. "The group's doing great," Nick briefed me. "The kids think Tristan is a god; they'll do anything he says!"

Tristan was one of the male field instructors on the opposite shift. He had a similar style to most of the other male instructors at that time, a strategy of leadership that was basically that of the alpha male: *You will do what I say because I'm smarter and stronger than you, and any power struggle you get into with me, you're going to lose, period.* Tristan's strategy of leadership involved getting into power control battles with the kids, and winning them.

Nick was happy, he slept much better at night knowing that the kids were safe and under control. But there was something about this style of leadership that bothered me, and Nick had summed it up perfectly: "The kids think Tristan is a god."

Short term, it worked great, but what about the long term goals? Did we want to teach kids to blindly obey any authority? To follow the strongest and smartest leader regardless of where they were being led? Or did we want to teach them to think for themselves and increasingly make their own choices as they stepped more and more into adulthood?

When I began my third shift with this group of eight boys, I vowed to never get into a power control battle with another kid ever again. I decided I never wanted to have another experience like what I'd had with Jill. So, for myself, I changed Monarch's teaching on power control battles to this: "Never get in a power control battle, but if you do get into a power control battle, get back out of it."

I became very good at never getting into power control battles, and just as good at noticing when I started to slip into one, so I could slip right back out. I realized that there is no power control battle unless I agree to take a side opposite from the other person. And why would I ever want to do that? Whenever a kid refused to do what I asked, I learned to restrain from firing a new and heavier round of ammunition, widening the gulf between us. Instead I would join them and get on *their* side. In fact, I never left their side; that was the whole reason I was there.

If a kid objected to an assignment I gave, I'd express genuine interest in their objection, asking, "Why don't you want to do the assignment?" Much of the time that simple question would let them know they were heard, and then they'd get on with it. If they did still have an objection, often it was pretty reasonable: "I'm too thirsty, I ran out of water on the hike and didn't refill at our last stop." "OK, go refill your water and then do the assignment." Often the objection would have nothing to do with the assignment at all: "I don't like where my tent's set up." Within reason, I'd do my best to accommodate their needs as long as it also met mine: that the boys and girls tents were separated far enough to meet policy, and any possible trouble-makers were separated or camped close to me.

Other times I'd join the kids a different way, yelling and stamping about in mock horror: "God, what a fucking awful assignment!" I'd say. "I can't think of a worse way to spend my time. I'd rather die and go to hell than write another one-page check-in. You want a check in, I'll give you a check in!" Then I'd just return to my tent. They'd comment about how crazy I was, but after my "tantrum," they'd often find it hard to get back to their original state of defiance, and they'd just do the assignment. Other times I'd exaggerate in the other direction, with a display of over-the-top enthusiasm: "You don't *have* to do this assignment," I'd say, "You *get* to do this assignment! You are the chosen ones! And what you write down will be passed on from generation to generation, teaching the ways of the student Zachary for seven times seven generations! And those students will have no need for parents, simply graduating from students into field instructors, for they will have the teachings of Zachary!"

Of course sometimes they would still just refuse—to write the assignment, to hike, to do their group chores, whatever. But now when they refused, I never took on their refusal as a reflection on *me*, and thus never assumed a position where the group might also see it as a reflection on me. This wasn't about me, it was all about them. If they didn't do the assignment, I explained that was their choice, and they could work it out with their therapist. Not doing the hike was also a choice they could make, which would mean our group wouldn't make it to our next camp. Not doing group chores was another choice they could make, which had its own consequences with the group. Often I would completely delete myself from the situation, which immediately eliminated a lot of resistance. When I truly realized that nothing was about me, suddenly everything was easy. I didn't have to prove *anything*. I was here to support the kids, not coerce them.

Even with very intense confrontations, I never again experienced a need to enter into a power control battle. It may be difficult to believe, but it's true—and that's what much of this book is about. It's also extremely important to realize that most confrontations never got to the point of great intensity. If I had a lot of stories of huge conflicts and confrontations to share with you, that would be a sign that the methods I used weren't very effective. I have some stories of major conflicts—I wasn't perfect—and you can read about how I managed them, but you'll see that the true proof of the tools I have to offer lies in their ability to set the stage so that conflict is worked through long before things get dangerous or damaging. There's only so much you can do when you find yourself in the path of an avalanche, but there are endless things you can do to make sure you never put yourself there in the first place.

So here I was, more than two years after I started work at Monarch, standing in my boss's office having just heard Nick tell me that when he first hired me he didn't think I'd last beyond my first expedition. Nick shook his head and looked me in the eyes as he said, "I couldn't have been more wrong about you. When you were out in the field, I *always* slept well. After you worked a few expeditions, I knew that no matter what crazy shit went down, you'd handle it. I'm gonna miss you, man."

"I'm gonna miss you too," I said, deeply touched by Nicks appreciation.

But I was still taken aback. This was the first I'd heard that he initially never thought I'd survive at Monarch. Suddenly a new perspective fell together in my mind. I saw the male instructors that Nick had hired before me—the classic alpha male mountain man type. Then I saw the male leaders Nick had hired after me—softer spoken men about whom I'd initially held similar doubts as to their ability to lead a group of rowdy kids. Had I inadvertently shifted the culture of leadership at Monarch?

Of course the answer to that question really isn't important. What's important is that it is possible to lead both gently and firmly. It takes time and dedication to build relationships on an equal level with challenging kids, but if you care enough to do this, you will have influence that is greater than the most fearsome alpha male, and it will be the kind of influence that will continue to guide them throughout their lives, long after you've gone.

After implementing the specific, practical tools in this book, you may be surprised to find your group more or less leading themselves, replacing "Lord of the Flies" with a small community showing genuine respect and support for each other. The following pages are filled with story after story from my experience demonstrating exactly how to achieve this kind of success with any kids. Because if it can be done with a bunch of teens who are forced to be in a place they hate, it can be done anywhere, whether on a wilderness trip, in the classroom, or at home with your own children. Whether you are a parent, a teacher, a youth leader, or a human being wanting to connect with and support the teens in your life, may this book offer you an enjoyable roadmap on the journey.

Chapter One

My First Expedition

I grew up with the Rocky Mountain wilderness at my back door, climbing trees and cliffs with my brothers to heights that most parents would have found hard to watch. But to my brothers and I it was freedom and conquering new challenges each day, and our parents taught us to assess each situation and be realistic about what we could handle, and what the risks might be if we were wrong. I learned to backpack and camp, and I led various back-country expeditions for my college, including several month-long trips. The wilderness has always been a part of me.

But then the trips started to get just a little boring. Wandering around in the wilderness with a bunch of privileged youth was all well and good, but what was our purpose here? What was the greater meaning? I wanted to work with the challenges of under-privileged kids, or at-risk youth. I wanted to work with kids who were challenged or unhappy in their lives, and show them how much joy there is to be found in wild things, and each other.

The Monarch program met all the above criteria except one: the teens were very privileged. For roughly a decade the

Trailhead Wilderness School had been a wilderness therapy program for adjudicated youth (court ordered), but when public funding dried up, they were forced to switch over to being a private program. They changed their name to Monarch, and they had to charge full price to participants. That's when I became a field instructor, and I was soon to find that though many problems are fixed by money, many others are not.

I was asked to come in a day before my first three-week shift, so I could shadow the outgoing staff and get a day of training before officially starting. When I showed up I was introduced to K-less (Ric without a "K", he explained). He thanked me for showing up to replace him a day early, threw his bags in his truck, and took off. "Have a good shift!" he said.

So I guess by "shadowing," they really meant "substituting." My new boss Nick didn't say anything, and he didn't give any hint that anything had changed, so I didn't question him about the apparent change of plans.

"All right," he said, "You ready?" I nodded, hoping that I was.

Nick drove me just outside of Georgetown CO, where we hiked into the Mountains and met up with the group—eight boys camping out with K-less' co-instructor Molly. Molly had a big smile and a great laugh. She wasn't much more than five feet tall, but I could see she was strong. "You're not leaving too, are you?" I asked, only half joking.

"No," I'm here one more night, I'll show you the ropes. "It's really a great group right now."

I was surprised when several of the kids came up to me of their own accord. They looked me in the eye and shook my hand, introducing themselves and welcoming me to the group. This was *not* the image of at-risk youth I'd expected to meet on my first day at work.

That night Molly introduced me to the field paperwork, showing me how to write the daily student evaluations, when to fill out incident and accident reports, how to give out the students' meds (and keep them locked up at all times).

The next day Molly wished me well and took off, replaced by Deryn, my co-instructor for the up-coming expedition. Deryn was tall and thin, with long dark hair and freckles. That first night we lit a fire and I experienced my first "Group" with the kids—an opportunity for anyone to air grievances and resolve conflicts, or for kids to get support in their own process of being in the program. This particular group focused on one of the boys, who recounted his recent therapy session with his parents. He talked about his struggle back home. On the one hand there were his friends who were into drugs, and his own desire to continue using, and on the other hand his parents were afraid for him and intolerant of any drug use. Deryn was so passionate as she spoke with the kids; her care and devotion to their support was obvious.

The next night Deryn asked for a night off to visit her dog, who was really sick. So on my second evening of work, I found myself working solo. We built a fire and had another Group, and it went well. I learned more about the kids, and one kid, a small red-haired boy named Jesse, really opened up about his feelings and struggles at home. My heart went out to him, and it felt really good that I could be here to support Jesse on his difficult path to a better home life.

After the group, Jesse asked me if he could borrow a headlamp to use back at his tent to journal about home, and what he'd told us in group (they weren't ordinarily allowed headlamps at night, as a precaution against run-away attempts). I let Jesse have the headlamp, wanting to encourage his growth.

The next morning I had a nervous feeling in my stomach. Surely Jesse hadn't run away, I told myself. He didn't seem the type, and it was a high-functioning group. But I *had* broken Monarch's general guidelines by giving him the light. I got up and immediately woke up the kids. Thankfully, Jesse was still there in his tent. He got out bleary-eyed and returned the headlamp. After breakfast Casey approached me and told me he thought Jesse had manipulated me into giving him the headlamp.

"I thought it was appropriate, Casey," I said, "since Jesse used the headlamp to journal." But I knew Casey was right. I was just lucky that my first lesson in manipulation probably resulted in nothing worse than Jesse staying up late reading a comic book in his tent. I realized that it was important for me to get to know the kids much better before giving out favors.

We collapsed our tents and packed up everything in our backpacks, and when Deryn arrived we started the expedition, hiking deeper into the pine-covered mountains. Jovus, the biggest, strongest kid in the group, lagged behind from the beginning, needing constant encouragement. He stopped constantly, holding up the group.

"There's this little bird on my shoulder that tells me I'm worthless and I can't do it," he moped from beneath his mop of hair.

Our first night in the backcountry Casey got sick and threw up in camp, so I dug a hole in the ground and cleaned up the mess to prevent an epidemic from sweeping through camp. We took a rest day the next day, which Jovus appreciated, and it was enough time for Casey to get over his stomach flu.

The next day we hiked farther and higher up into the mountains. It was March in the Rockies, and soon the dirt trail became lost under 3-4 feet of snow. We had to strap on snowshoes to keep hiking, and with our backpacks on, it was no easy task. Being one of the heaviest of us, Jovus' steps would often punch through the snowpack and he'd sink in up to his knees, or even his waist. His snowshoes were too small for him, so he was "post-holing" regularly, whining in frustration and driven to the point of collapse as more snow started to fall. When one of his snowshoes broke, we decided to make camp. We set up our tents on the snow—something I'd never done before. Everyone went straight to their sleeping bags after dinner because it was so cold; we didn't make them stay up for a Group.

Washing dishes in the ice-cold water at night was the worst kind of finger-aching cold, but it was satisfying to learn that I could comfortably camp in the snow. (Only later, when I truly warmed up at home after the expedition, would I realize that the trip gave me partial nerve damage in my toes due to poor circulation over a prolonged period of time. Since then I learned to never go to sleep before fully warming my toes.)

When Deryn did the nightly check-in over satellite phone, reporting that our group was safe, there was a message waiting for her that her dog had died. That night when I got up to pee, I heard her soft crying from inside her tent.

The following day we had another rest day while we waited for Paul to come in and relieve Deryn so she could go and bury her dog. The kids took turns sledding down a short hill and going over a small jump they'd built at the bottom. All except for Sebastian, a kid who was there for gambling problems who seemed to always be in a good mood (maybe because he'd always gambled with his parents' money). Sebastian was an overweight openly gay boy who commented from the sidelines in stereotypical fashion: "Oooh, that was a *big* one, Casey! Big air! Do it again, do it again!"

When Paul showed up, Deryn said goodbye, and we hiked deeper into the mountains as the snow deepened beneath us and continued to fall from above. When we finally reached the head of the valley, Paul gave an avalanche safety lesson, in preparation for the next day when we would hike up above tree line and over a ridge. Paul was young, like me, with long blond hair and a firm presence and wisdom with the kids that I really admired. He was also full of energy.

When we made camp Paul said, "I'm going to build a big circular bench down into the snow. We'll have our Group there, with a fire burning on the snow island in the middle! While I'm doing that, why don't you grab a couple kids and do the bear hang."

The "bear hang" was Monarch slang, not for hanging bears, but for hanging all our food out of reach of bears and other scavengers. Ideally we tried to get the food at least ten feet up in the air, and five feet out from the trunk of the tree. I found the most amazing bear hang location I'd ever seen. A spruce trunk had fallen and caught in the fork of another evergreen about twenty-five feet up. The end of the spruce had splintered off when it fell, leaving about fifteen feet of bare trunk protruding horizontally from the forked tree.

Sebastian and Casey gathered all the duffle bags of food from the other kids, and they helped me toss the rope up over the horizontal trunk, we tied on all the food duffels, and I started to haul on the rope. With the friction over the trunk above, I couldn't lift ten people's food by myself.

"Help me out," I said.

"I'll help pull on your rope any day!" Sebastian said.

"Good," I said, ignoring the innuendo. "Let's do this."

We hauled on the rope, and suddenly the tree trunk gave way with a sharp CRACK from above. The boys dived one way, I went the other, as a ten-foot section of the trunk lanced downward like a battering ram with a jagged, splintered end. It skewered the snow right where we'd been standing moments before, protruding from the snowpack like a giant toothpick in a marshmallow.

"Holy shit!" Sebastian exclaimed. "That nearly got our asses!"

We gathered up the food and looked for a hanging spot that wasn't likely to kill us. When we got back to Paul, he had a wonderful fire blazing on a snow island in the midst of his circular snow bench.

"How'd it go?" he asked, as we joined him and the others around the fire.

"Well," I said, "I found out why these youth are at risk!" And I told him the story.

When the fire had melted its way down into the snow and put itself out, the kids had already retreated to their tents for the night. "Supervision is pretty easy in the snow," Paul said. "If we're not hiking, all they want to do is get warm in their tents. Keeping them within eyesight and earshot at all times takes a bit more managing in the heat of summer."

As I'd soon enough find out.

But this was a high-functioning group of boys that just wanted to curl up in their sleeping bags to get away from the cold.

The next day we snow-shoed up above tree line, over a saddle completely smoothed over by thick blankets of snow. Jovus was having trouble again, so Paul stayed back with him, hiking at his pace while I went ahead with the rest of the group. The landscape was beautiful as we crested the saddle, completely white and flat, and so bright it was hard to see even the packed snow beneath our snowshoes.

"Stop! Everyone stop!" I said suddenly, glad I was at the front of the group. Only a few paces ahead, the white surface of the snow ended abruptly in empty space, difficult to see against the backdrop of snow in the valley far below. We backed up and skirted to the side where we began to make our way over the saddle and down the far side. Looking back we saw the huge cornice we had begun to walk out on. A figure appeared on top, walking straight for the treacherous, overhanging edge.

It was Paul.

The rest of the group and I started waving our arms and yelling, "Go back! Go back!" But with the distance and wind, Paul couldn't hear us. He was right at the lip of the cornice now, and I wondered if the whole thing might give way under his weight, carrying him down onto the cliffs below. He backed up, and skirted the cornice. When he regrouped with us he told us he hadn't seen the edge until he was right up on it, and he'd felt the snow groan and shift under his weight.

Now that we were past that danger, all we had to worry about was avoiding an avalanche as we descended below the saddle, then traverse across a scree slope so steep that it was closer to being a cliff. I could see right away that one tumble here would mean certain death. At least the slope was south-facing, so most of the snow had been burned away, but the path was very narrow, more of a goat trail through the loose rock. Hundreds of feet below, cars crawled along I-70 like bugs.

I took a breath, remembering how unsteady Jovus and some of the other kids had been under the weight of their winter backpacks. Now their snowshoes were strapped onto the load as well, adding not only weight, but bulk. As we headed forward, the trail was intermittently covered over by snowfields, where Paul or I would have to kick footholds into the slick surface for the kids to cross.

We successfully traversed the gauntlet above I-70, disappearing back into the safety of the trees, and after a few more nights, it was the end of my first expedition. At shift exchange Paul and I updated the incoming staff on each of the kids, then said our goodbyes. Paul pretty much had to tear me away from the group.

"All right," he said, "It's time to go."

I got home to find that my girlfriend hadn't wasted any time finding someone who wouldn't be gone for three weeks straight every three weeks. My toes had warmed up at that point, and they were going through a cycle of burning, then turning completely numb. I was worried the nerve damage might never heal, but I had no second thoughts about my new employment.

Chapter Two

The Trip that Lives in Infamy

My first expedition had a high-functioning group of kids, and the leadership challenges all involved the cold and dangerous conditions of the outdoor environment. The group itself was great.

This chapter is about a different kind of group—one that I led about a year later after I had much more experience—and the compounding challenges that can present themselves. This was a trip about life and nearly about death, precipitating a nasty lawsuit. This trip required me and my co-instructors to be not only wilderness teachers and guides, but also makeshift therapists, parents, and first responders.

I came on shift just after the group had finished up individual therapy and group therapy with their families during "family week," in Georgetown. I hiked into camp in the mountains outside Georgetown along with Zach, with whom I'd be leading the expedition. Zach was a strong, stocky, dark-haired guy who'd just finished school at a Buddhist university in Boulder. He talked with a slow meditative quality, like he was feeling into each word he spoke. This was Zach's first night as a field instructor, and he was not about to have the same high-functioning kind of group that I got on my first expedition.

The first thing I noticed as we came into camp and took over the shift was that the boys and girls tents were not as separated as I liked to have them (we had a co-ed group this time). Monarch was a small program, ideally with two separate groups of eight kids, each led by a different set of field instructors at different expedition locations. But Monarch rarely ended up with exactly eight boys and eight girls. This meant there was usually one group of either all boys or all girls, and a second co-ed group. The co-ed group often worked out great, and sometimes made things a lot more interesting.

This expedition there were only twelve kids total in the program. Since there was a policy of two staff-members per group, in situations like this Monarch would often combine the kids into one group with three staff members (thus saving the expense of paying a fourth staff member). It helped with the budget and kept the required ratio of one staff to four kids. But if you've ever done this kind of work, you know that a group of twelve kids is far more difficult to manage than a group of eight, no matter how many extra staff you have. In fact, having extra staff can have its own logistical challenges of keeping each staff member on the same page. Zach and I were going to drive all twelve kids down to our expedition site in New Mexico, where a third instructor would meet us before we started our backpacking trip through the Bandelier National Monument.

Back to the tents. One thing I never compromised on was that *I* decided where each kid set up his or her tent. If I didn't like a dynamic between two kids, I made sure they set up apart from each other. If a kid didn't seem to be very cooperative, I'd have them set up right near me. I never told the kids why I set them up where I set them up, that would just be asking for trouble (and probably they already knew at some level, if not all levels; they were troubled, perhaps, but not stupid). If kids asked me why I made them set up in a particular configuration,

I'd say, "Because I'm crazy and I don't know better," or I'd point out a dead tree that might crush them in the night if there was a wind storm. If a kid asked me why I kept having him set up near me every night, I'd say, "Because you're my favorite." The kids are smart about these things; they know why you're doing what you're doing. No need to waste time talking about what everyone already knows, and giving them something to argue with. My actions showed them that I was paying attention and not letting anything slide. And often kids were thankful for my arrangements of camp, because it helped them get distance from dynamics they would have felt trapped in otherwise.

So as Zach and I walked into camp, I noticed that the girls and boys tents weren't as far apart as I liked. Actually, the girls and boys camps were far enough apart, but one of the boys, Toby, had set up his tent out on the flat of a dirt road that passed by both camps. He was a new kid I hadn't met yet, so I wasn't about to have my first sentence to him be, "Move your tent."

When the outgoing staff took off, I introduced myself to Toby. He was a skinny kid with even skinnier jeans that he was constantly having to pull up so as not to reveal too much of his ass crack. I asked him why he was here. Drug use. Not caring about school. His eyes were downcast, as he kicked at the dirt. A streak of his black hair was dyed red, and his ears were pierced, though the earrings had been removed.

"You're probably not too happy to be here, huh?" I said.

"Nope."

"Well I realize it's no vacation, but even so, a lot of us end up having fun despite the fact that it sucks to be here. Anyway I'm here to support you in getting back home."

"Sure, whatever."

"One thing I'd like you to do tonight is move your tent off the road and set it up over here with the rest of boys camp," I pointed out a spot.

He looked up at me, "But I already have it set up over there, the other leaders were fine with it there!"

"Yep, you're right. And I'd like you to move it over here."

"But it's flatter over there."

"It's flat enough here too. Do you want me to help you move it, or do you have it on your own?"

"Huh! I can do it if you want to just make my life more difficult for no reason. This place sucks!"

Supervision was the other reason I had the kids set up their tents where *I* wanted them. I needed to keep the kids within eyesight and earshot at all times, (unless they were in their tents, or one of them specifically got permission to use the latrine or pee in the woods). If I let them set up anywhere, it would make my job of keeping an eye on them a hundred times harder. I always took extra time to set up camp to make things easy for me for the rest of the day.

So Toby moved his tent, we had dinner, and after dinner Toby and Amelia were off a little ways from the rest of the group, within eyesight, but having a low conversation I couldn't hear. Private conversations are also something we didn't allow as a general rule.

"Toby and Amelia," I said. "Come on and join us over here."

"We're having a private conversation about her therapy and my therapy," Toby said.

"Then it can be heard by the whole group, or it doesn't need to be said," I replied. "Everyone here is going through therapy, and everyone can support you and relate to what you're going through. You're all in the same boat in many ways." They came and joined the group, clearly annoyed. I don't ask that kids like what I tell them, just that they do it.

Here's where, if they said "no," I wouldn't threaten them and get into a power struggle, I'd just walk over and ask them what they needed. I always took the approach of finding out what the kids needed, recognizing that, and meeting that as much as possible within the parameters of our rules around safety and group openness. By never once stepping into the false role that I can somehow control the kids, I completely freed myself from any loss of power if a kid decided not to do what I asked.

Amelia glared at me. She'd been diagnosed with clinical depression and placed on Lexapro and Abilify. She'd dabbled in marijuana, drinking, cutting herself—not an uncommon profile for a girl at Monarch. She stuck her hands in her pockets, letting her field pants slouch to reveal the matching tattoos of guns on her hip bones.

"Nice guns!" I said.

"Yeah, that's why my parents sent me here."

"If I got a tattoo of guns, what would you recommend for my hip type?" I asked.

She burst out laughing.

Pretty soon I circled up all twelve of the kids and held our first group with Zach and I as leaders. I asked them to share how their therapy had gone, what they had learned or struggled with, and how things were going with the group. How could we make it an even better group that everyone wanted to be a part of? I was always looking to meet their needs wherever I could, to find out what they truly wanted and support that in happening to the best of my ability.

"I don't have anything to say," Christina said. She was a precocious blonde 14-year-old who had been put on suicide watch a few nights ago because of her threats to kill herself.

"That's OK, Christina."

Other kids shared about their experience, or how they thought the group could improve. After a while I turned to Kaylie, a girl who not only hadn't shared anything, but was standing almost outside the circle, eyes downcast, her body language very disengaged from the group.

"What about you, Kaylie, do you want to share anything, you look pretty unhappy," I reflected back what I'd noticed. I did my best to show the kids that I was paying attention to all of them, not just the louder ones who demanded attention.

Kaylie burst out into tears and started telling us how much she missed her family, how much she didn't want to be here—a lot of the usual stuff kids go through when they find themselves suddenly whisked away to a Wilderness program.

"Thanks for letting us know, Kaylie. I think a lot of the kids here feel or have felt the way you do. Is that true?"

As I looked around the group, other kids nodded and shared their own experiences of homesickness and sadness. The kids were always a bigger—and better—resource than I could ever be.

"I wouldn't like being sent here either," I said, "and I *like* the wilderness. Luckily there's no rule that says you have to like it here. What I can tell you is I'm absolutely here to support you in figuring things out with your parents so you can get back home as soon as possible."

"I don't want your support!" Kaylie said, "I want out of here."

"Well if you change your mind, I'm here. And I'm guessing other members of the group would be happy to support you too." A few of the other kids nodded or chimed in with agreement.

We closed with our nightly check-out ritual. We did a variation on rose and thorn (everyone sharing their "high" and "low" from the day) adding a bud and leaf (a hope for the coming days, and something each person would like to improve upon).

I asked Zach to see the other kids to their tents while I stayed with Christina. When Zach returned I turned to Christina. "OK," I said, "Let's get you ready for bed too."

Suicide watch meant I had to first check that Christina's tent had nothing in it but her sleeping bag. Then she'd strip down to her long underwear and get in. The purpose of this was to ensure that she had nothing with which to cut or strangle herself—sharp rocks, tent stakes, twine or a necklace. We were also making it as hard as possible for her to run away. Ideally a female would oversee this process, but our third staff member, Kelly, wouldn't be joining us until we got to New Mexico.

With Christina zipped in her tent, and all her stuff (including her shoes) in my care, I set up my tent door-to-door with hers. Then I tied her tent zippers together out of her reach, and tied this to my tent zipper so I'd hear her if she tried to get out in the night. As additional precaution, Zach set up his tent on the other side of her, as per Monarch's suicide watch policy. If Christina needed to use the bathroom, she would have to wake one of us up to do it.

Thankfully most teens have an incredible capacity to hold their pee when they're warm in a sleeping bag and the only bathroom is a tree out in the cold where wild animals lurk.

Before Zach and I went to sleep, we did our own personal check-in, a daily practice that I learned should not be avoided, even if you think you have nothing to check in about. Often it's the only time that staff members have alone, and even if I don't think I have anything to say, I learned it's important to make the space for it. After taking a breath and stepping aside with my co-instructor, I would almost invariably find something come to me that *was* important to say, so that we'd both stay on the same page as leaders, and ensure that our own needs were being met. Sometimes it was just my own time to vent with my co-instructor. And if I truly had nothing to say, I could only know by allowing the space to check in away from the kids, and even then usually my co-instructor would have something important to say.

During our first check-in, Zach told me how impressed he was with how I worked with the kids in a way that was both effective and honoring their experience. It made me look back over the previous year from a broader perspective, and helped me appreciate how much I'd learned through trial and error from each expedition.

The next day as we drove down to New Mexico, Toby became the center of a new problem. The previous leaders had agreed to let his parents buy a whole load of candy for the group to go crazy on during the drive down, but because Toby's parents had bought the candy, Toby began taking ownership of the candy. He became its de facto custodian, doling it out as he saw fit. This may seem trivial at first glance, but on a wilderness trip where bagels, quick oatmeal, and dried beans are the primary food source, having control over candy gives status and power. Until Toby became a clear ally, there was no way I was going to let him have that kind of power in the group. "This Candy is obviously causing disagreements," I said. "We don't need to have it, it is a privilege, after all. If it just makes things more difficult, we can go without it."

"No, no. The other leaders said we could have it!"

"And I'm sure they would do the same thing as I am if they saw it was causing trouble. If you want to keep the privilege of the candy then I'll be the one to give it out fairly, and if it causes any more trouble, then no more candy." I took the candy and gave it out myself, in a fair and just manner.

When we got to Bandelier, we had a nice day exploring the ruins of the pueblo peoples who once lived in the desert canyons there. But as we explored the cave dwellings, once again I noticed Toby and Amelia always together, and always lagging behind the group. I was constantly telling them to come along and stay in sight, which got to be a nuisance with ten other kids to keep track of. Counting heads became an unconscious reflex. By the afternoon, there was some obvious tension and bickering amongst the kids, so we stopped and had a Group. Ben was particularly upset by all the "drama." When I asked Ben what he meant by "drama," he said he didn't like the cliques that were forming, nor the group conflict. He wanted the group to be more united and working together so they could finish the expedition in a positive way and earn their overnights with their families. What I didn't know at the time, and would discover in a few days, was that Ben hadn't revealed the full extent of what was bothering him.

The next day Kelly, our third staff member, arrived with an unanticipated additional student, Cathy, so I got to count heads up to thirteen. As I often joked, it was good to know what the plan was, so that you'd at least know one thing that *wasn't* going to happen. Flexibility and change was how it worked. A new student was ready to come in, so in she came. All sixteen of us packed up our backpacks, left the pueblo ruins behind, and headed into the Bandelier back country.

Having Kelly there to help with the larger group was fabulous. She took over tying her tent to Christina's every night, which meant that one of the three of us could actually set up somewhere else. We were in the back country again, where everything was simplified to what we could carry on our backs, and no one could deny their own role in the function (or dysfunction) of the group. Our wilderness family was small enough that no one could escape noticing the effects he or she had on the rest of us, whether for good or bad. This was one of the greatest teachings of these wilderness trips. Life could be heaven or life could be hell, and it pretty much depended on how well we got along and worked together. In the complexity of the modern world it can be hard to see how we affect each other, but in the intimacy of a small group in the wilderness it is hard to ignore.

Our first morning in the back country we awoke to ten inches of snow on our tents. Some tents had collapsed or broken poles under the weight. That morning Christina's therapist left a message saying we could take Christina off suicide watch, which was nice because it meant we wouldn't have to give Christina's daily updates over the satellite phone, which didn't always work when we were down in the bottom of a canyon. It was hard enough getting service to last long enough to simply call in our location, and that the group was safe.

After fixing the broken tent poles and eating breakfast, we headed deeper into the wilderness. The new student, Cathy, lagged the whole way, so our pace was slow. As the trail began its descent into a deep canyon, the sheer drop made Cathy stop all together.

"I'm afraid of heights," she said anxiously, keeping as far away from the edge as possible. When kids said things like this, it was always a question whether they were sincere, or just manipulating. Sometimes it was both. In general I preferred taking kids at their word, unless I had reason to think otherwise. If I found a solution to a "fake" problem, it was just as useful as finding a solution to a real one—it was still a solution. Sometimes it was my sincere offer to help that solved the problem; other times it was their unwillingness to admit that they were faking.

But in this case Cathy looked sincerely afraid, this wasn't a conscious ploy to get out of hiking. So I stepped into unofficial therapist role and guided her through the NLP fast phobia cure.* I'd already used the technique successfully with one of my co-instructors to cure her phobias of heights and then again for lightning—two issues that we had an opportunity to test out immediately in the same expedition. After guiding Cathy through the short process, I invited her to cautiously take a look over the edge. I wanted to test out that it had worked, but I also knew that a lot of fear comes from not knowing what's there. Fear often comes more from creating a scary picture in your mind, than from what's actually there. When she looked over the edge she seemed to gain confidence, and she was fine the rest of the way down into the canyon.

The next morning Ben requested that we hold a Group; he was even more nervous than he'd been before. He said he didn't want there to be so much drama, and so many secrets. He wanted to earn his overnights with his family next week, and he worried that if the secrets continued, none of the kids would be trusted to leave the field for time alone with their parents. That was when we learned what all the "drama" was truly about. Toby had slept with Amelia, and not just once, but several times. Starting on the previous expedition, he'd snuck out at night on several occasions.

Right then and there Kelly met one-on-one with Amelia, and I met with Toby, giving them no opportunity to agree on a story to tell us.

"I'm sorry," Toby told me, shaking his head. "I'm so sorry."

"Did you use a condom?" I asked.

"No."

"Was there full penetration?"

"Yes."

"Did you come inside her?"

"Yes."

It looked like I was going to be tied to Toby's tent now, for quite a few nights. And Kelly would get to know Amelia a lot better.

---

* To learn more about NLP visit: www.MarkAndreas.com

In these situations, (indeed most situations) the teaching has pretty much already happened. There isn't a whole lot left to say.

"You realize she might be pregnant now, and we're a couple days from the trailhead?"

"Yeah, I know, it was stupid."

"There are STD's to think about too, you might want to get tested the next time you have a chance."

If all went well we could hike out in one and a half days, that way if she and her parents decided to, Amelia could somewhat reduce the chances of a pregnancy by taking the morning after pill.

But things did not go well. Cathy hiked more and more slowly, she stopped eating, and she started throwing up. We knew Cathy had a history of anorexia, so we'd been watching her food intake carefully during the trip, making sure she ate enough. Now we didn't know what was going on. She was clearly ill; she wasn't throwing up on purpose.

"Go on without me," she said over and over, not realizing how ridiculous that sounded. We were on the trail the entire day, because of how slowly she went. Since we were in the desert, we had to get to our next camp for water.

For the last couple miles Zach had to carry Cathy slung over his back, and I carried Zach's backpack on my chest. The rest of the group stepped it up, taking turns with Cathy's pack. We made it into camp just as night was falling. Zach gave Cathy some Gatorade to rehydrate, I tied my tent to Toby's, and we all went gratefully to sleep.

At about 5am Zach woke me up. "I haven't slept at all yet," Zach said. "Cathy's been throwing up all night. I need you to take over so I can get a little sleep."

I got up and stayed with Cathy while she threw up into a plastic zip-lock bag.

"I need to go to the bathroom," she said weakly.

"Alright, just walk a few paces over there and I'll turn around," I said.

She walked shakily away from her tent and I turned around. After a minute without another noise, I said, "Cathy? How's it going?"

No response.

I turned around. She'd walked about 30 ft. before fainting. She lay sprawled on the ground, a head-sized boulder right by her neck where she'd collapsed.

Oh, no! I thought, running over to her. Though she was probably fine, I hadn't actually seen her fall. If her C-7 vertebra—the most delicate neck vertebrae—had actually struck that rock on her fall, then she could have a spinal injury. It was pretty much the only way an otherwise healthy teen could damage their spine by simply fainting on flat ground. I grabbed her head in my hands, stabilizing it against the ground as her eyes fluttered open.

"Stay still," I said, filling her in on my guesses when she asked what happened. I called Kelly over to help, thankful that my Wilderness First Responder training was fresh in my memory after having taken a recertification course just a few weeks earlier. Kelly and I stabilized Cathy's spine and rolled her onto one side, slipping a pad under her before rolling her back. That would keep her warm while I did a full assessment, which wasn't made easy by the fact that she kept throwing up. Kelly and I would roll her to keep her spine straight, and she'd spew. She had long since expelled all food from her stomach, and now it was clear fluid mixed with a dark brown. Was it blood? I wasn't sure.

Between the bouts of vomiting, I continued with the assessment: heart rate, respiratory rate, pupils—while Kelly took notes. When Kelly squeezed Cathy's toes and I asked Cathy to tell me which of her toes was being squeezed, she got it all wrong. Then she threw up again. She had a distracting condition (the vomiting) and she couldn't accurately tell me which toes I was squeezing, which meant we couldn't clear her to walk out on her own.

By now Zach had begun sprinting up out of the canyon with a cell phone. (Our satellite phone wasn't working down in the canyon, but we knew there was cell service at the rim.) We were still a good three miles from the trailhead at the nearest road.

Cathy was getting really scared. "It hurts!" she screamed, sobbing as she threw up again. "I have to sit up, now!"

I couldn't let her bend her spine, but I could tell by her voice tone that she was going to try whether I liked it or not, so I got her into a clamshell stabilization with one of my forearms running along her spine to the back of her head, the other forearm up the center of her chest, my hands forming a kind of c-collar around her neck. Then I lifted up her torso and Kelly held the bag as she threw up more dark brown.

"I'm dying, I'm dying, I'm dying!" Cathy moaned—and I wondered if she was right.

All we could do was keep her warm, keep her spine stabilized, and track her vital signs on a piece of notebook paper every ten minutes while we waited for Zach to call out for help.

I was amazed how quickly help came. Though Zach had been clear that the vomiting was unrelated to Cathy's possible spinal/head injury, any time those two are mentioned in the same paragraph to a search and rescue team, they *move*. It only took the team from the volunteer fire department several hours to get in. They strapped Cathy to a backboard with the piece of paper containing our scrawled notes, and took her away.

Kelly went out with Cathy, leaving Zach and I once again supervising 12 kids. When Nick showed up he brought along two more staff, and a little 12-year-old kid, David. Nick introduced David to the group, and we circled up. We were still waiting to hear back from Kelly who'd gone with Cathy to the hospital. Part way through our Group, David asked to go use the outhouse in the campground where we were staying.

"Sure, David," Nick said. Nick had taken David's shoes to discourage him from trying to make a dash for it. Nick told us that the kid had been surveying the road atlas during the entire drive down, asking a lot of not-so-veiled questions about the distance to the nearest town. Being a small 12-year-old, David's field pants were several sizes too big for him, which served him rather well to keep his socks clean, because the pant legs completely enveloped his feet, trailing behind him like two limp wind socks as he went to do his business.

David disappeared into the outhouse, and our Group continued. Minutes later the outhouse door slammed and we looked up to see David running away at full speed into the heart of the desert wilderness, his trailing pant legs flapping behind him like flags of freedom.

Nick and Zach took off after David, but Nick was in his down booties, so Zach took the lead in his flip-flops. David was fast for a kid in over-sized pants. Zach jumped logs and dodged trees to catch up with David before the poor kid lost himself in a place where, on his own, he would likely die of dehydration before finding any sign of civilization. When Zach caught up to David, he yelled, "David, stop!"

David stopped dead in his tracks, the wind gone out of his sails (or pants). At that moment Zach's foot caught on a branch and he went down face first into the dirt at David's feet. Zach jumped back up, but David didn't make a second attempt at escape. Zach brushed himself off, and escorted David back to the group.

That evening the therapists arrived, and the next day Cathy was released from the hospital and let back into the field. We learned that she had been undernourished since before she started the trip with us, due to her eating disorder at home. The sudden increase in physical exercise had exacerbated her malnutrition. It was a *very* good thing she'd gone to the hospital. Her spine was fine, as I had suspected, but her electrolytes had dropped so low that her heart actually was within risk of stopping. Now she had a whole supply of Gatorade to keep her electrolytes up—which was the envy of all the other students.

Needless to say, Zach and I were ready for a break at the end of this expedition!

When Amelia's pregnancy test came up positive, her parents were opposed to her getting an abortion, so Amelia brought her baby to term and put it up for adoption, and Amelia's parents brought a lawsuit against Monarch. Thankfully, Zach and I were not involved, as we had carefully followed Monarch policy in everything we did. Amelia's pregnancy wasn't an outcome that any of us wanted—not her, not her parents, and certainly not any of the staff. When Zach and I debriefed the trip, we looked back with an eye for what we could learn from the experience. I logged away all the nonverbal cues I could remember that might, in the future, give me a clue that something wasn't right. Zach and I also submitted an improvement to the suicide watch policy to allow for greater supervision of the rest of the group while continuing to give the same level of attention to any kid at risk of suicide.

Amelia's mom was outraged that a wilderness program would ever have kids in a position where they could have sex. I understand her concern, and I don't know what her expectations were for the program, or how clearly the realities of the field were communicated to her. I wasn't a part of that conversation.

What I do know is that if her goals were to prevent her daughter from having sex, she could have sent Amelia to a lockdown facility. I found out later that Amelia admitted to having more than ten sexual partners by the time she was fifteen. Her choice to have sex with Toby was not a symptom of carelessness on Monarch's part. Yes, we want to set our kids up for success, providing them with an environment that supports good choices. But if we take away all choice, that's not therapy, that's prison. Sadly, there are a lot of prisons for kids that do just that, but that's no solution. The reality is that if we want our children to have the opportunity to grow, it necessarily involves risk, including the risk that they might make mistakes—sometimes even big mistakes. What makes sense is to provide a structured and supportive environment where kids' needs are being attended to, where they are allowed to be human and make choices, and where their mistakes are noticed and addressed in a supportive learning process.

It could have been a valuable experience for Amelia to have her parents join in this process with Monarch, helping her see the natural consequences of her choices, and learn from the experience. Instead they chose to be a different kind of model to their daughter, showing her: "When you make a mistake, we are going to find someone else to blame, and sue them."

Partly prompted by the lawsuit, an article in Westword magazine painted Monarch as a boot-camp style Wilderness program that was unsupportive and punishing. I would not have worked there for more than two years if that had been true. I'm not saying Monarch was perfect by any stretch. In tense and difficult situations, we all have our moments of gracelessness, staff as well as students. We're all in the learning process. But in my experience, Monarch was a place of unusual compassion and support, for the kids as well as for the staff. My impression from talking with other staff is that Monarch was unusual in its approach of expressing kindness and compassion while helping kids develop communication and life skills. Many other programs did in fact operate like boot camps, based primarily on punishment and force, but Monarch was not one of them.

After the Westword article was published online, several students, including Cathy, wrote comments detailing how positive and transformational their experience at Monarch had been for them. Cathy made some of the best friends of her life at Monarch, and the program changed her life. I wish I could include word-for-word, what she and some of the other kids wrote, but for reasons unknown to me, the comments have all been taken down.

Certainly not all kids would say they had a positive experience at Monarch. When you're starting with kids who are forced by their parents to be somewhere they don't want to be, you have your work cut out for you. Most kids were very happy when they got to leave Monarch and return home, and that's the way it should be. But most of the kids also left expressing an appreciation for skills and experiences they gained from Monarch. Wilderness therapy, I discovered, is not so much about the therapy, as about the *experience*, for which there is no substitute.

One student, after leaving Monarch, went right back into the hard drugs he'd been doing before. When he hit rock bottom, he remembered his experiences of group support and friendship at Monarch. He cleaned up his act and got a Monarch tattoo as a touchstone for his new path in life—not the butterfly though, some things are just too girly; he got a crown.

Chapter Three

The Trip from the Hall of Fame

It was late October when I came on shift, and Nick warned me about a new kid, Brandon. "He's classic adjudicated," Nick said, "He reminds me of the kids we used to see a lot when we only took in court-ordered kids." Zach, who'd been one of the field instructors on the previous shift, told me that Brandon had put up constant resistance and defiance. "That kid is trouble," he told me.

So I made a particular effort to engage with Brandon from the beginning, and develop a relationship with him. He definitely had one of those tough-kid exteriors. His eyes were hard, and always slightly squinted as if in suspicion of the world. His body language was classic too. He liked to stand with his hands in his pants, spitting between his teeth as if he was chewing tobacco. When he looked at you he would clench his jaw and squint even narrower.

But I didn't assume he would be the same with me as he had been with other staff. Different people can bring out different elements of a person. Maybe Zach had reminded Brandon of someone problematic from his past. So I asked Brandon a lot about himself, searching for commonalities.

"Brandon, what brought you here?" I asked.

"Fucking up, I guess," he said. He had quite a past—abuse, neglectful parenting, drugs, in and out of facilities all his childhood. I never shied away from any subject, always asking with a genuine interest and care. If a kid chose not to tell me about something, I respected that, but I always asked, to show my interest. Behind Brandon's hard exterior I sensed something else. He seemed like a nice enough kid if you just ignored his body language.

It snowed a lot that first week, and the 7 boys in my group were happy enough to hike out of camp each day to go to therapy in Georgetown, where they got to be indoors and have access to tea and cookies. But getting them up out of their tents into the cold snow was sometimes a challenge.

One morning Brandon wasn't eager to get out of his warm sleeping bag and start the day, so after our first unsuccessful round of trying to wake him up, I told my co-instructor Jon that I was going to have some fun and impersonate a mountain lion. I snuck down near his tent and began making a strange huffing growling sound that I don't think sounds much like a mountain lion, but it's my best scary animal/alien noise. I stopped for a bit, then started again, growing louder. I figured that he'd snap out of sleep at the noise, then realize it was me messing around, and we'd have a good laugh. But it turned out a little differently.

"MARK!!" Brandon yelled, a clear tone of desperation and fear in his voice. "MARK, there's an ANIMAL!"

Hearing the sincere fear in his voice, I didn't have the heart to tell him it was just me. My goal wasn't to make him feel humiliated. So I snuck back away from his tent, and said, "What's up Brandon?" And I began walking audibly toward his tent.

"Mark, I think it was a *mountain lion*. Did you hear it?"

"What did you hear?" I asked.

"It was this growling. It was like right outside my tent!"

"Wow, I don't see anything now."

"Oh, my god, it was like right there! *Jesus*. You must have scared it away when you came over!"

"Well luckily they're pretty skittish if that's what it was. And mountain lions generally only hunt at night." This was a fact that I would reinforce whenever given the opportunity. A little fear never hurt to assist in keeping the kids in their tents at night when we field instructors had to get our own sleep.

"Well, time to start the day, Brandon. You ready to join the rest of us?"

"Yeah, yeah. I'll be right out."

Jon and I had a good laugh about it during our staff check-in that night when the kids were back in their tents. The next morning it had snowed ten inches on us overnight. The only indication of the kid's tents were white humps in the snow. They were very happy to be leaving Georgetown that morning, heading south to New Mexico to start the backcountry portion of our expedition for the next two weeks.

Soon I found myself back in Bandelier, climbing a reconstructed ladder up to one of the sacred Kivas used for ceremonies by the ancient pueblo people who built it. Jon was already up the ladder in the Kiva with the rest of the group. I was heading up the rear, with Brandon climbing up behind me.

"They should give field staff guns to protect against wild animals in the wilderness," Brandon said, obviously still troubled by his experience with the mountain lion in Colorado.

"You know, they used to issue us guns," I said with complete seriousness, "but not to protect against wild animals, to protect against the kids, and keep everyone in line."

"*Really?*" Brandon asked to my surprise, completely buying my tale.

As a kind of game, I had a habit of telling tall tales, or white lies. Things can get boring when you keep to the facts, so I would take opportunities like this to have some fun. Not just for me, but for the kids as well. This was a way to keep them engaged, and keep them guessing. I would do anything to keep them oriented toward me, wondering what crazy thing I might pull next. As long as I could maintain that, they'd be following my lead.

"Yeah," I said, "but they stopped issuing guns when I shot a student."

"You *shot* a student!" (It's amazing what kids will believe sometimes, maybe it's my innocent face.)

"Well, it wasn't on purpose," I said. "It actually happened right here. I was climbing up this ladder with my gun in one hand, and I slipped and BAM! I pulled the trigger and hit the kid right above me."

"Oh my god."

"Yeah, and he *died*."

"Woah!"

"Yeah, and his body hit mine and it was dominoes all the way down. Luckily for me, most of the group was below me, so they cushioned my fall." I turned back and looked Brandon in the eyes with a hint of drama in my voice. "I was the only one who made it back from that expedition alive."

Brandon squinted at me, a hint of a smile threatening to reveal itself, "There's no way that happened!"

"Well," I said. "Let's just say it's a good thing they took away my gun. I didn't *mean* any harm."

"You are so full of it!"

"Hey, be careful what you say. That was a hard thing for me to go through. I'm still sensitive about it." I reached the top of the ladder and stepped into the dark ceremonial cave, caked with generations of wood smoke.

We were all enjoying our time in the sacred space of the Kiva, when Brandon and Josh got on each other's nerves. Like many arguments, it started with something pretty inconsequential. Josh kept making comments in the voices of Beavis and Butt-head, and Brandon told him to stop, which Josh ignored.

Suddenly Brandon walked up to Josh. "If you don't shut it right now, I'm gonna *beat* your ass!" Brandon puffed out his chest, feet planted in a pose daring Josh to defy him.

This was a side of Brandon that I hadn't seen yet. Josh looked totally surprised, not sure what to do.

"Brandon, Josh!" I said in a loud voice, drawing their attention to me and away from each other to give me time to cross the Kiva to where they stood in their face-off. "Josh, go over there," I pointed to the other side of the room. First I just wanted to get them separated and cooled down before someone got hurt. We could work through the problem later. Josh went to the other side of the room, happy enough to have a way out. "Jon, will you take Josh and the rest of the group down out of the Kiva. Brandon and I will come down later."

"Yep," Jon said. "C'mon guys, time to head down."

By the time they were all out of the Kiva and back down on the ground outside, I had taken some time to empathize with Brandon, and I got his agreement not to pick a fight with Josh as long as I gave Brandon plenty of space away from Josh so his "annoying comments" wouldn't upset Brandon. Then we also climbed down out of the Kiva.

At the bottom of the ladder, I told the group. "Brandon obviously just got really upset at Josh. We'll have the time to talk this through in a Group. We could do that right here, but I'd rather do it back in camp. Is there anyone who's not OK with waiting until we get back in camp?"

Not surprisingly, everyone was OK with that.

"OK, great. I'm gonna ask that we all have a silent walk back to the van and a silent drive back to camp. I think we could probably all appreciate some quiet right now. Is everyone OK with that?"

I found that if I did the work all along the way to create a good group culture of kids who respected me, rarely would they have a problem with these sensible things I requested. With a fight about to break out, they were all happy to see that they had a leader who didn't hesitate to take control and keep everyone safe.

"OK, great," I said. "As long as everyone can keep that agreement to stay quiet until we get back, I think we'll all be happier doing Group back at camp." As much as possible, I would set these kinds of frames early and get agreement up front. Now if a kid decided to talk on the way back, I had a group agreement I could refer back to, instead of just asking for silence out of the blue. "And if anyone changes their mind," I added, "we can always do Group before we get back." This was not a threat, but a simple statement of fact that I was prepared to back up. Sometimes I would stop a van in the middle of a van ride and have a Group rather than let disrespectful dynamics continue. Unless someone had a good reason for a Group, kids generally avoided being the one "who started the Group before we got back to camp."

"OK great," I said, "Josh, why don't you go up at the front with Jon, and I'll hang back here with Brandon, that way you guys can have some time apart before our Group."

Back at camp Brandon had cooled off. Things would be easier now that he and Josh both had a bit of distance from the confrontation in the Kiva. I decided to run Group by teaching my simplified version of Marshall Rosenberg's basic Nonviolent Communication technique:

"Part of being in a small group like this, 24/7, is that there are going to be things one person does that gets on another person's nerves," I told the group. "That's why we have our solo time each day, because even if we don't realize it, having a break from everyone, and just having some time to ourselves, can be a really necessary thing."

"So before we check in with Brandon and Josh, I want to teach you guys a specific way to let someone else know that you're feeling bothered by something.

"I'll give you an example. Say I'm annoyed because my roommate keeps leaving clothes lying around our apartment and I like having a clean living space. So instead of just saying, 'You asshole, stop leaving your things around,' which probably won't get their cooperation, there's a more respectful way I can ask them to change. I do this by breaking it down into these four steps: One, *observation*; Two, *'I feel bad;'* Three, *need*, and Four, *request*.

"So in my example I'd say to my roommate, 'I observe that there are a lot of clothes lying around the house.' That's the Observation, next we go onto the feeling bad: 'When I see this I *feel* bad.' Now we say our need: 'Because I have a need for a clean living space.' And our request: 'So my Request is that you keep your things picked up.'* Now, my roommate can agree to my request or not, that's his choice. But now he has the choice, because now he knows how I feel when things are left around the house.

"So Brandon, you got pretty upset about something back there, but this group is for everyone, and we all have our things that annoy us, and our ways we'd like the group to work better. So would anyone like to express anything at all to the group, using observation, I feel bad, need, request? I'll help you along as you go."

"Sure, I'll try it," Abe said. He was a bigger kid with curly hair who'd been sent to Monarch because of his obsession with Halo. He'd gotten so good at the video game that he'd played in some major online tournaments. "My Halo name is Ghost, with a zero instead of the letter 'o,' " he later told me. Apparently if you were into Halo, you knew that name. From the sound of it Abe might have been able to support himself as a professional Halo player, but his mom didn't like the idea. (The other thing his mom was famous for not liking was Johnny Depp, whom she apparently dated and then dumped.) Abe was one of Brandon's buds. They'd connected over chess, and rarely did a day pass without them breaking out the travel set they'd brought along.

"All right, here goes," Abe said. "I observed you guys almost get in a fight. Um, what's next?"

"Feeling bad or annoyed."

---

* To read my article about modifying Rosenberg's Nonviolent Communication method for more simplicity, see my blog post "NVC and the Value of a Single Word" on my coaching website www.markandreas.com

"OK, yeah. So that made me feel bad, because, um, what next?"

"What's your need?"

"Because I have a need that I'd like to be a part of a group that doesn't have fighting. And so, yeah, and so my *request* is that there not be any fighting."

"Thanks, Abe. Way to jump in there and give it a go. So Brandon, that's a request that you can decide to agree to or not, it's up to you. What do you say?"

"Yeah, I'm cool with that, Abe. I don't need to fight."

"I know that something got you pretty upset back there, Brandon," I said, "and I'm wondering if you want to say anything about that to Josh or the group?"

"No, I don't have anything to say. It's over," Brandon said. "It's not a big deal."

"OK. I get that its' not a big deal to you right now. At the same time, stepping into Josh's shoes, I would have felt pretty threatened. Josh, do you want to say anything to Brandon?"

"Brandon, I was pretty surprised. I thought you were gonna beat my ass. So I'm just glad you didn't beat me up, man, 'cause I know I would've lost."

"Brandon," I said. "Can you stay in contact with Josh while he's talking to you?" Brandon looked up and met Josh's eyes. *Contact,* is the Gestalt Therapy word we used at Monarch to mean not only eye contact, but also really listening and taking in what someone else is communicating.

"Yeah man," Josh said. "I'm glad you didn't beat me up. 'Cause I'm not a fighter."

"Thanks Josh," I said, feeling protective of the kid and how vulnerable he was being. But I had to protect Josh in a way that wouldn't come down hard on Brandon; that would be counter-productive. At the same time I also couldn't let any of Brandon's behavior slide. Especially not for something as serious as threatening another kid in our group.

"Josh, is there anything you want to say to Brandon, about what you need, to feel safe in the group?"

"I'd just like to know that you won't hurt me," Josh said, a pretty reasonable request. I didn't bother having him put it into NVC language.

"Yeah, man. I won't hurt you. I already said it's over."

"Thanks Brandon, I appreciate your commitment to Josh. I also get that it's over for you, and at the same time, when someone's threatened in the group sometimes it takes a bit of time to build back trust.

"For all of you, the whole group, my job is to keep you *all* safe. So now I'll say something with NVC: Brandon when I saw you threaten to fight Josh, I felt bad, because I have a need to keep everyone in this group safe. So my request to you, Brandon, is that next time instead of threatening another group member, you instead come to me for support in getting what you need."

"Yeah, all right," Brandon spit on the ground.

"Can you make contact with me, please?" He looked up and met my eyes. "Thanks. Is there anything specifically that you need so that next time you won't even get to a point of wanting to physically fight?"

Brandon shook his head and clenched his teeth, "I guess sometimes I just need some space."

"OK, great. I understand that completely. If you're not getting the space you need, will you come to me?"

Brandon scrunched up his lips and nodded.

"Great, because if there's one thing there's plenty of out here in the wilderness, it's space. Do you have a request of Josh in terms of space?"

Brandon looked across the circle at Josh. "Josh, sometimes you just talk a lot, and I get tired of all the impersonations, but if that happens I'll just hang back. I can get my own space."

"Great, Brandon. I appreciate you noticing what you need and how to get it for yourself. Josh, do you need anything more to feel safe in the group?"

Josh shook his head.

"Josh, I'm sorry man," Brandon said. "I got carried away. I won't do that again."

Josh nodded, "It's OK man. I just want us to all get along."

"Does anyone else in the group have anything else to say?" I asked. "I'm here to support you all in having the best experience out here as possible, and in getting back home as soon as possible, and in order for that to happen it's important that we all keep each other safe."

No one else had anything to say, so that was the end of Group. Of course Groups don't all work out so well. So I want to let you know what I'd do if the kids weren't so agreeable, which was fairly often.

At the most basic level, I'm noticing and calling attention to the reality of the situation, and not requiring that it be anything else. There is no sense in demanding that kids shake hands if they clearly aren't over the problem. In the above scenario, the important elements are to give Brandon nothing to fight, and show Josh that I'm making sure he'll be protected in the group. Since Josh is the weaker party, I'm particularly careful to watch his body language, align with his need for safety, and make sure he feels it.

If Brandon hadn't looked Josh and me in the eyes, hadn't apologized sincerely, or hadn't been willing to engage with us, just insisting that it was "over," I'd say something like this to Brandon:

"I realize it's over for you, and the fact is that other people in the group felt their safety threatened, and I'm not OK with anyone being threatened in this group. So until we can be in contact with each other as a group, until *everyone* in the group is satisfied about how we're going to work together, I'm going to ask you to be on solo so you don't have to be with the group until you're ready."

Solo meant a kid would set up their tent away from the rest of the group, and not be in contact with the rest of the group. This was a very useful leadership tool, and it was important that it never be thought of as a punishment, but as a *solution*. Often kids hated solo and thus were motivated to re-connect and rejoin the group. However, other kids found solo a great relief where they could get much needed time with their own process, and then come back into the group when they were ready.

The rest of the expedition went without another threat from Brandon, or any of the other kids, and Brandon never showed me anything but good humor. When he discovered that I write Science Fiction and Fantasy he got really excited, and in his free time he started writing a fantasy novel on lined notebook paper, which he asked me to read for feedback. When we hiked into the backcountry our fun really began as a group. Yes, we had our quarrels as always. I'd usually stop the group right there and then and address it before things became more than a minor issue, and soon we'd be back on our way hiking along the trail.

I would often pass the time telling riddles and five-minute mysteries that the kids would try to solve: "A man is found dead in a room with 53 bicycles, why?" Then they'd spend a lot more than five minutes asking yes or no questions to figure out the answer. I had a *lot* of riddles to tell, saved up over the years. Only on one expedition did the kids exhaust my entire supply of riddles.

At one point I threw in my own five-minute mystery: "Now this actually happened to me, so listen closely." (And this story actually *did* happen to me). "So I was out hiking with my friend—on a trail much like this one, in fact—when all of a sudden we came upon a *dead* person lying there in the trail. My friend and I knelt down and took a close look, even touched the dead person. Then we left without calling the police or notifying the authorities. Why?"

"Because the authorities were already there?" Kyle ventured.

"No, it was just me, my friend, and the dead person."

"This didn't really happen, you're making it up!" Brandon said.

"No, I absolutely swear to you, it happened, and you might want to figure out why before it gets dark tonight!"

"He's gonna kill us all in our sleep!" Kevin shouted.

"Yeah, right," Abe said. "Was it an open casket?"

"Out along a hiking trail in the mountains? No sir!"

It went on for some time before they pieced together that the "dead person" was not what you ordinarily think of, but someone's ashes that had been placed near an overlook inside a heart made of stones.

It was nice for the guys to be in a group where there wasn't the distraction of girls, and also where they could really push themselves physically—we had long hiking days, and even did some challenging off-trail hiking in order to summit a small peak. When we got deeper into the desert we found big, ripe, prickly pear fruit growing on the cactus. I plucked one of the purple fruits and carefully scraped it with a small rock to remove the spines. Then I cracked it open and sucked out the purple juice and seeds.

"Mmmmm!" I said. "Too bad none of you are allowed to eat any of this, it's against policy." (This was actually true, but I wanted them to have a full experience of the wilderness and all its offerings).

"Oh man. Can we just try a little?" Sander asked.

"I must insist that you CAN'T HAVE ANY, policy is policy."

The kids all looked at me trying to read my intentions, curious to taste a prickly pear. I was telling them "no," but my body language all said "Yes!"

After a bit of back and forth, pretty soon they caught on: "I'm definitely not eating any prickly-pear over here!" Sander said, trying to figure out how to pick one of the spiky things. "Everything to policy. Ow, ow!"

Pretty soon all the boy's hands were stained purple and full of tiny cactus stickers.

"I gah one in mah tongue," Sander said, and then he started using the purple juice to paint his face.

We were in the deepest desert on Halloween night. When we got into camp Jon and I broke out the candy we'd secreted in without the kid's knowing. "We're gonna trick-or-treat tonight," we told them. "Here's how it's gonna work. During your solo time before dinner you all have a chance to get creative and make yourself a costume out of your limited backpacking supplies and what you find around you. At the end of the evening, the best costumes will win candy!"

With candy on the line, the kids got incredibly creative. Sander was the ninja-turtle Leonardo. He drew a six-pack onto his green T-shirt with a sharpie, then cut the sleeves off to make his green mask. He also wore a green bandana over his hair, and his turtle-shell was a green and brown plaid long-sleeve shirt stuffed with other clothing and tied onto his back. His swords were two curved sticks.

Brandon was a non-turtle ninja, covered from head to toe in black, with just a slit for his eyes. Abe was a "retard," wearing his clothes all wrong and his glasses upside-down. Definitely not PC, but it didn't offend anyone present, so while I didn't encourage it, I also didn't see any benefit in me cramping his particular style that night.

Josh and his good buddy Rustin played gay lovers, wearing their underwear outside their long underwear, and sharing a red shirt between them that they'd split down the middle. They made use of the sharpie too. One's shirt said "pitcher" and the other's said "catcher." They named themselves Enis and Jack. They kept things above board for the most part, and had a fabulous time.

Finally, Chris was a zombie. He ripped his shirt to shreds that hung off his body, rubbed dirt in his long hair until it stuck out at all angles, and smeared more dirt on his face.

Matt was the only kid that didn't dress up.

And of course Jon and I weren't going to lose out on the fun. The dressing up thing was a last-minute idea, so we didn't have anything special prepared for ourselves. I happened to have a pair of boxers with American flags, so I wore those over my blue long underwear, used a red fleece for a cape, and a white balaclava over my head along with a red bandana and a headlamp. I was Wilderness Captain America, and I even had one red and one blue Nalgene water bottle dangling from each side of my belt.

Jon dressed up as "confused," which was totally awesome. He wore a baseball hat with *two* brims that said "which way??"

on it. And he managed to get his torso *inside* his own backpack, his legs sticking out the bottom, so that someone else could actually put him on and wear him. Since Matt didn't have a costume, he wore Jon for the photo.

But the best part was yet to come. Jon and I took our places atop a huge boulder in the middle of camp. As Wilderness Captain America and "confused" we held the candy aloft and our ghoulish subjects were in awe.

"Dance!" We shouted. "Who so ever dances the most vigorously shall get candy thrown upon him!"

And they danced.

And we pelted them with candy.

And they yowled with pleasure at each impact, scrambling for the wayward treats as fast as they could before jumping up and dancing another mad jig to provoke more of our sweet missiles. You've never seen kids so happy to receive a pelting. It was good therapy for all of us.

The next day we left our tents pitched and started a day hike to an incredible cave that had been a sacred site for the pueblo peoples. The shallow cave was inaccessible without a ladder, perched up in the cliff for all to see the intricate variety of painted hands and symbols in reds, whites, blacks, and yellows.

Rather than just go check out this awesome piece of art, I told Jon I wanted to do something a little different, and he agreed. A quarter mile before we arrived at the cave, I told our group that we were about to see the artwork left over from a civilization lost to the distant past, yet this artwork still remained after so many years for all of us to see. I asked them all to close their eyes and imagine their own lives moving forward, the things they would do and see, until their whole life span had completed. Then I asked them to think about what they wanted people to remember about them after they were gone?

I told them to open their eyes, and asked them to stay quiet with their own thoughts as we walked the remaining distance to the cave. At the cave I invited them each to find a spot to sit alone and journal about what they hoped would remain of themselves after their bodies had passed away. Their journal entries ranged from deep to dismal, but I think the change of pace and perspective was worth something to each one of them. It's important to include not only the silly and profane, but also the sacred—both irreverence and respect. I value expressing myself with a range of human qualities, and having the freedom to step into different roles in different parts of my life. I want my kids to also have a full range of colors with which to paint their life stories.

On our hike back we took a rest break in the shade by a stream. Brandon and Abe got out their magnetic chess set and started a match. After we refilled our water and had some snacks, one of the other kids picked a horsetail growing near by. Droplets fell from the picked end like water from a straw. He flicked it at another kid, who picked a horsetail and flicked horsetail water back at the first. Another kid picked a horsetail, and for some reason he meowed when he flicked its water at a nearby target. Soon Jon and I and the other kids were all grabbing handfuls of horsetails, jumping and dodging over packs as we flicked the horsetails at each other, meowing like a cat in heat with every spray. All except for Brandon and Abe, who remained absorbed in their chess game, oblivious to the horsetail-cat-battle that raged all around them.

These were teenage boys, remember, with peer pressure oozing from their pores and the desire to be cool as a number-one value. I often think of this memory as an example of how much fun can be had when the space is given for it. When judgment and coolness can be laid aside and we can all just *be*. It was a precious moment. When there is group trust and respect, there's no end of joy possible with imagination and a few horsetails.

And at the end of my shift, Brandon hadn't once given me the least show of the disrespect that I'd been warned about.

SECTION II: Tools

I want to acknowledge that many of the following tools were taught to me in Monarch's top rate field-instructor training. Many more of them I learned from other teachers and mentors, or from my own direct experience. All of them are tried and tested techniques that work.

Foundational Principles

1.

If it ain't fun, you ain't doin' it right!!!

Most of the time out in the field, we were having fun. Kids like to have fun, and if you're having fun, you're not getting into (too much) trouble. If I gave you all the examples of the various ways we had fun, it would fill a book in itself. The kids don't even need to be having fun, as long as you're having fun (never at their expense) in a way that invites them to join you if they choose. If they don't choose to join you for the moment, *you* still have fun as a leader. Soon most of them will join you. People, and especially kids, like having fun.

The ways we had fun were endless. In snow we built snow forts, in the summer we dammed the creek. Some kids got into building the most amazing latrines, complete with rocks for back-rest, seat, and arm rests. We held competitions for best creative adaptation of clothing, and fastest tent set-up. We played mind-games and riddles on the hikes, told ghost stories and jokes, and tried to give Jessie a dreadlock. We participated in the time-honored arts of "Who can melt a quesadilla on a stick," "Who can hit that weird-looking tree with a rock," and "Who can blow on a coal until it gets completely red."

Once my boss Nick and I showed up at 5am at a kid's home to wake her up and bring her to Monarch, since her parents were worried she'd run away if they tried to take her themselves. So her parents showed Nick and I downstairs to their daughter Nita's room. We woke her up and Nick said, "You're coming with us."

"Oh no, seriously? Fo real? Yo, this's gotta be a joke!" She was the whitest kid in the whitest town in Colorado, but she spoke like she was from the 'hood. Nita was into hip hop and break-dancing. For the next 6 hours I drove her out to meet up with the rest of the group in the Sand Dunes.

"Yo, this ain't too unexpected," she said on the drive.

"Well I've got a lot of time to answer your questions, so ask away."

"Fo sho, fo sho," she said, nodding her head.

Later on around the campfire I made up a rap in her honor, from one white brotha' to his white sista.' Between verses I did vocal percussion into my hands, demonstrating my catastrophic beat-boxing ability, and during verses I played some chords on my co-instructor's backpacker guitar to back up my rapping:

"Yo yo, yo! This is Nita's rap! Fo-sho!
It was five in the morning I was rubbin' my eyes,
When I woke up in my room there were two strange guys,
They told me they would take me to a place I would despise,
'Cause I was doin' drugs, and also tellin' lies!

It's the Monarch Center for Family Healin'
Where we're down with Contact and expressin' feelin'
Forever through the rugged Rocky Mountains we will roam,
'Cause once you are among us you ain't never goin' home!
Awww nah... You ain't never goin' home!"

The kids all thought this was so hilarious (including Nita) that when I came back on shift 3-weeks later, they had taught it to the new kids.

2.

Frame everything in their interests

Whether you're a teacher, a wilderness leader, or a parent, odds are you didn't get into this for the pay. So this really is all about the kids. That's the truth, so make sure you frame it that way when communicating with them.

Alex was a new kid in my group who I was told was a run risk based on his history, so I kept a close eye on him any time I stopped the van for gas or bathroom breaks on our way down to Arizona where we would have our expedition. On our first night camping out in the field I went over to his tent and said, "Hey Alex, do you need to go pee or anything before you're ready for the night?"

"No, I'm good."

"OK, I'd like to hold on to your shoes for the night."

"Seriously, you're going to take my shoes?"

"Yeah, I know it must be pretty annoying. I'd be annoyed if I were in your place. It may not make a difference to you, but I want you to know that I'm doing it because I want to keep you safe, and I want you to stick around with us. I think you're a pretty cool guy, and I'd be sorry if I woke up to find you weren't here in the morning. I also want to let you know that my job out here is to support you as much as possible in graduating from this program and going home where no one's going to be messing with your shoes."

"Yeah, I get it. They probably told you how I've run away from other programs in the past."

"I appreciate your understanding. And I sincerely hope this is the last program you ever have to be in."

Everything you ever do, no matter what the boundary or expectation, is about the kids' interests. That's the whole reason you're here.

3.

Power control battles:
(Never get into one, but if you do, get back out of it)

T his approach is all about recognizing the true facts on the ground, and giving up any attempts to bluff or fake having more power than you actually have (which puts you at risk of being challenged). Give up all need to control the other person, and your true power is secure. That's all the power you'll ever need in this job, assuming your goals are to be a decent human being who doesn't try to manipulate others into doing things they don't want to do.

A good mantra to keep you on track is, "I can't (and don't want to) choose what you do, I can (and will) choose only what I do." Kids may choose to cuss me out, I may choose to realize it isn't about me. They may choose to threaten me, I may choose to call the police. They may choose to hate me, I may choose to take their shoes at night until I'm convinced they are no longer a run risk.

In addition to living this truth, it can also be useful to verbally express it to the kids (as long as you're really living it):

"Jason, I can't choose what you do, and even if I could I wouldn't want to. That isn't what this place is about. I can only choose what I do. You get to choose what you do. And all of the choices I make I'll be doing my best to support you."

The last sentence makes it clear that there is no threat here. I am fully honoring the kid, and their ability to choose. Saying, "I can only choose what I do; you get to choose what you do," makes it very clear that I am confident in my own choices, and consider myself to have options no matter what the kid might choose to do. This is a powerful statement. There is no threat, I'm acknowledging their autonomy (which often gained me huge respect), *and* they see that I'm comfortable with them making whatever choice they decide to make.

Leaving my own choices (how I might respond to a kid's violation of my requests and expectations) unspoken was often particularly effective with kids trying to push me. There are times when you do want to tell kids exactly how you will respond if they disregard your requests or expectations. But there are other times when doing this can sound like a threat, and it's going to work best to leave them wondering: "Mark can only choose what he will do... hmmm... what might that be? He seems to feel comfortable that he's got plenty of choices no matter what I do. Maybe I shouldn't test him. Maybe I should just do what he's asking."

So it's important as a leader to go through contingency plans for all the worst possible scenarios and find reasonable choices you can be comfortable making when kids do test you, as they inevitably will. We had staff training on how and when to physically restrain kids, with role-play scenarios where we attempted to restrain each other (and got first hand experience of how difficult that is). We were trained in ways to protect ourselves from physical violence, when to call the police, when to let a kid just do their thing and focus on protecting the group, etc. When you've practiced and thought through all these possibilities ahead of time, you are in a very secure position to be there for an emotional teenage kid trying to throw you off balance.

WAYS TO STAY OUT OF POWER CONTROL BATTLES

Meet needs: See all defiance as expression of a need that is not being met, and ask how you can meet that need (without compromising group needs): "OK, what is it you need so you can feel good about participating in the group chores?" or "What don't you like about the assignment? Is there a different assignment you'd rather do that would still meet your therapist's goals?" or "What is it you don't like about camping here? I may not be able to satisfy everything you're wanting, but I'll do my best within Monarch policy." At the most basic, "What is it you need or want that you're not getting?"

Everyone makes their own choices: As discussed above, recognize that kids can and will make their own choices, and that is a *good* thing. If a kid still refuses to do any therapy assignment, you can say something like, "OK, that's a choice you can make. I respect that; this place certainly isn't about me making all your choices for you. I ask that you stay quiet so as not to disturb the others while they are doing their assignments. At the end of the expedition you can work things out with your therapist. I'd even be happy to help you talk with your therapist, if you want. Who knows, maybe there's a way you can get assignments that you don't feel are worthless." Or "Gregg, I understand you're choosing to refuse to set up your tent anywhere else. This spot you've chosen is too close to the girl's camp according to Monarch policy, and I have a job to adhere to Monarch policy. If you're going to stay here, I'm going to ask all the girls to move so we're within policy, and you'll be on solo not interacting with the group until you're ready to abide by the rules of camp that everyone has agreed to, which are in place to benefit all of us."

Align with the group: "Samantha is choosing not to cooperate, I just want to let you all know that as long as the rest of us still cooperate and work together as a group, each of you will still earn all your overnight visits with your family at the end of the expedition. I know it can make it more difficult when one member of the group isn't participating, and I apologize for that, and I'm here to do everything I can to make this as positive of a group as possible for those of you wanting to participate and achieve your goals of getting back home as soon as possible." If you have the group's respect, you have your power as a leader. If you've laid the right groundwork ahead of time, and shown yourself to be a positive, just, and supportive leader, my experience is that the group will always side with you, not the troubled student who is acting out. If you frame the situation as I did above, often the rest of the group will naturally start functioning better, distancing themselves from the dysfunctional element.

WAYS TO GET BACK OUT OF A POWER CONTROL BATTLE WHEN YOU NOTICE YOURSELF SLIPPING INTO ONE

Admit your error: We all make mistakes. Whenever a kid points out one of my mistakes, and I realize they are right, I agree with them. "You know what, actually I agree with you, Tony. I screwed up there. There's actually no way I can make you do your chore, and even if there was a way I wouldn't want to. I didn't start working here so I could boss kids around, I'm here so I can support you in making good choices for you. So I'm sorry I said it in a way that made it sound like I was trying to make you do it, and I hope you'll still choose to do your group chores so we can all benefit as a group." Countless times I diffused arguments and gained kids' respect by doing this. They felt heard and were satisfied, and we could move on. By doing this I am also modeling the behavior that I hope they will adopt—noticing their own mistakes and being able to admit them and learn from them and move on without it being such a big deal.

Once I was really angry because three kids had run off at night while we were sleeping. All three had come back, but then the girl, Dawn, spooked, knowing she'd broken a major rule that might jeopardize everything she'd been working toward with her family. It was night and she ran for it again. Unlike most expeditions, this time we were at the beginning of a service project in New Orleans rather than safe in the isolation of the wilderness. Dawn darted out the front door of the building in which we were staying. I bolted after her, but when I hit the street she was lost in the shadows; I couldn't see which direction she'd gone. I chose a direction, but I was wrong. By the next day she still hadn't come back. I held a Group, feeling very protective of the 14-year-old girl alone somewhere in the city, and I made the mistake of blaming the boys for her disappearance. "Do you two realize what kind of danger she's in now?" I said. "She could be raped, taken advantage of, I hope you realize the choice you made isn't just about you." I could see their eyes harden and I realized I made a mistake. I took a breath. "I'm sorry," I said. "I was wrong to blame you two for Dawn's choices. You two made your own choices, which will have their own consequences, and Dawn made her own choices. What's going on for me right now is I'm really concerned about Dawn, I hope she's OK, and I wish she were here with us right now. I was wrong to suggest that it was the fault of the two of you." It can be easy to fall into the trap of feeling like once you say something, you have to stick to whatever you said to maintain your integrity. This is foolish, especially if what you said is foolish, which happens to all of us.

Redefine: "Whoohoo! You guys made it a whole two miles in seven hours! Get ready for the Olympics!" I said once after a particularly agonizing crawl along the hiking trail between camps. "Stop disrespecting us!" Marla snapped at me. "Just 'cause it's easy for you doesn't mean it's easy for us. Two miles is a long way for some of us, you say yourself all the time it doesn't matter how fast we go, as long as we keep moving, and we kept moving!" Marla gave me a perfect opportunity to redefine the meaning of my communication: "I'm sorry, Marla, I never meant to disrespect you or anyone in the group. I agree that the group mostly kept the breaks to reasonable lengths today, and kept moving at a steady pace. I guess when I was joking about our hiking pace what I was really trying to say is that I believe you all are strong enough to hike faster and have all the benefits— such as extra free time—of getting into camp sooner. I hope you guys get to experience that by the end of the expedition."

Admit your error even if there was no error: If what you said still makes perfect sense to you, it's often way easier just to admit you were wrong and re-phrase what you're asking in a way that gets the response you're looking for from the kid (rather than trying to explain how what you said actually means what you meant, rather than what they understood). This can be a surprisingly difficult thing to do, when we believe that what we said *was right all along!* But the goal isn't to prove that you were right all along, the goal is to get the response that makes your life (and theirs) easy. In the field of NLP, this is the presupposition, "The meaning of your communication is the response you get." It doesn't matter what was intended, what matters is what was received. Life and leadership becomes a lot easier when you realize you can *always* say, "Sorry, I was wrong about that, what I really meant to say is _____," even in situations when you were right to begin with. Once I was teaching map reading, when one of the kids said, "Mark, you said there were 100 feet between contours, but I checked and there are only 40." Now I'm sure I never said that, but does it matter? That's what his experience was. "Well if I said that, I was definitely wrong," I said, "because you're right, there are 40 feet between contours. It means there could be a 39-foot cliff that was invisible to us on the map, if it happened to be just in the right place between contours." Simply admitting error and moving on can be a lot simpler and easier.

One of my biggest sources of freedom and power as a leader was realizing that I never had to stick to anything I said. I could say anything, try anything. The important thing was to notice, what is the response I'm getting back from the kids? I paid close attention to this feedback, to know if I needed to amend, redefine, re-phrase, or admit error about anything I said.

"But surely there are some power struggles that you have to win," you might be thinking? Perhaps so, but I never found one. Teaching kids is not a war zone. I was taught how to physically restrain a kid, which is a very physical power control battle, but in all my time at Monarch I never needed to use it. Often kids were too big or strong to consider a restraint, so my co-instructors and I would find another way. And when kids were small enough for a restraint, we also found other ways.

See the Introduction, "The Key to it All," for a story of a power control battle I didn't get out of, and Chapter Four, "The Wall," and Chapter Five, "Damage Control," for stories of dealing with really defiant kids.

4.

There is no *need* or *have to*

OK, so it sounds great on paper to just say, "Take the kid's side and don't ever get into a power control battle," but what if the kid refuses to do something you need them to do?

First, any time you hear yourself say "need" or "have to" in relation to you or one of your kids either doing or not doing something, re-examine that thought. Do you really *need* to make it to the next camp? Do you *have* to stay on schedule? Do you *need* the new kid to listen to you? Do you *have* to teach them to respect you? Is it more important to make it to the awesome waterfall or address the conflicts and relationship dynamics holding up the group? Is it more important to change a kid into better behavior (presupposition: there is something inherently wrong with you that I need to fix) or is it more important to give them the space and opportunity to become who they choose (presupposition: you are inherently OK)? There is nothing, and I really mean *nothing*, that you or your kids ever *need* or *have* to do. There are consequences to everything, but nothing *needs* to happen.

I may have a need for human connection, but I don't *need* Tom to like me, or *have to* make Tom like me (so that we connect). This is a confusion between what we think will meet the need (I want Tom to like me) with the need itself (I have a need for human connection). Fortunately there are more people in the world than Tom, and thus many ways of satisfying the need for human connection. (And in this case it's possible for me to experience connection with Tom even if/when he doesn't like me!) We all have needs (food, water, shelter, safety), but we have many choices about what we do or don't do to meet those needs. We don't ever *need* or *have to* do any one particular thing, or have someone else do any one particular thing. If we get trapped into thinking so, it is a rigid stance that will actually serve to drastically reduce the amount of times that we get our needs met. In their bestselling book "Getting to Yes" Roger Fisher and William Ury talk about how getting away from "positions" (specific things we *feel* we need to do or have others do) to underlying "interests" (of which needs are the most fundamental) allows us to discover lots of possibilities for win-win resolutions of conflicts that will meet everyone's actual needs.

So first change "I need," and "you have to," to "I want," and "I request," This creates relationship rather than the disconnection of commander and commanded: "Johnny, I realize you don't want to be here, and I will really appreciate it if you decide to hike, because I'd really like to get into our next camp where we can be out of lightning danger, and I think the rest of the group would really appreciate that too. Is there some way I can help make the hike easier for you?"

If he still refuses, I haven't lost, because I haven't set myself up for a power control battle. Instead I've recognized his choice in the matter, and I've asked for his help. Whether he gives it or not is up to him.

I've also described his cooperation in terms of *his* wellbeing, staying safe from lightning and maintaining a good relationship with the group. I've included that I'll appreciate it too, even though this may be the last thing on a kid's list of importance.

But what if, no matter what you try, the kid refuses to budge and lightning is approaching? Easy, get the rest of the group to safety and leave Johnny to his chosen fate. In the end, we only have control over ourselves. To think that I should be able to control someone else will only set me up for failure. Focusing on what *I* can do, sets me up for success. The basic deal is this: you only have a problem if you hold yourself up to an unrealistic expectation of what a single human being is capable of. To paraphrase the Dalai Lama: "If you have a problem you can do something about, you don't have a problem. If you have a problem you can't do anything about, you don't have a problem."

5.

Natural and logical consequences

J ust as you don't need to invent *needs* or *have to's*, you also don't need to invent arbitrary consequences or punishment for kids who mess up. Not only is punishment no fun for either party involved, it is also ineffective, distracting the victim of the punishment from the true learning opportunity provided by their mistake (for more about why punishment is ineffective, see the post script to this tool).

Instead of punishment, we can first direct kids' attention to the natural consequences of their actions. In a small group surviving together in the wilderness, these consequences are made wonderfully immediate and concrete (one of the major benefits of wilderness therapy) yet they are present in any context. In tool 4 above, I brought up some of the possible natural consequences of Johnny not hiking: lightning danger and frustration from other group members who want to get warm and dry in camp. These environmental and social consequences are the two main categories of *natural consequences*.

In addition to letting the natural consequences do the teaching, there are times when creating a logical consequence makes sense. A *logical consequence* is one that is created by you, but fits logically with the transgression. We have a rule at Monarch that we keep a clean camp. So when students would leave things out overnight, I'd often collect them. The next morning I'd hide them and we'd play a treasure hunt for their things that had to be completed before we left camp. This was one logical consequence that I created to teach the clean camp rule (while also having fun, which is a great state for learning).

What's logical about a treasure hunt, you may ask? Every rule at Monarch is in place for the benefit of the individual and the group as a whole, which I'm happy to explain to students. The clean camp rule is to prevent loss of our supplies from wind or simply losing track of them, to prevent animals from coming into camp, and to have a nice living environment. Logical consequences are a great teaching tool any time the natural consequence might be too harsh for the individual (You lost your mug, so now you have to eat your beans and rice with your hands) or any time the natural consequence would have too negative an affect on the rest of the group (We have to wait for a day while Jaden figures out how to carve herself a new bowl out of wood). While experiential learning is great, there are many things I'm glad I never had to learn by direct experience, such as contracting hanta virus because I left my dirty mug out overnight for a mouse to poop in.

Sometimes I'd collect the mugs kids left out and fill them with dirt or pine cones, or the dirty pair of socks they forgot about. When they found it and complained I'd just shake my head at the strange things animals did in these parts of the woods, and then I'd give them some soap to clean out their mugs. Sometimes I'd leave everything where it was. It was amazing how long it could take kids to find their own things right where they had left them. These were logical consequences I created that taught the kids to be more aware of their things and where they left them if they wanted to get into the next camp on time.

In general the day's hike wouldn't be shortened if we got off to a late start. I was usually happy to hike at night, which had the advantage of being cooler in summer and gave me a good ambiance for making up ghost stories. The variations on the "find your possessions" game were also very enjoyable games for me to watch. It's always nice when natural and logical consequences are fun for you as the leader. The more you can show the kids that you are completely comfortable and self-sufficient no matter what they do—that you are happy hiking or not hiking—the less they will have any manipulative influence over you.

Refusing to clean the pot for cooking the group dinners had its own logical consequence: "All right Kevin, you can eat bagels and trail mix for dinner until you're ready to participate in the group chores necessary for a nice hot meal." I would then ask if another kid is willing to clean the pot for Kevin, in exchange for Kevin doing one of their chores when he decided to enter back into the group. Whenever a kid refused to participate fully in the group, we asked them to go on solo, separating their tent physically away from the group, and asking that there be no dialogue with group members until they were ready to rejoin the group. The group was something that kids were a part of fully, or not at all. There was no choosing what parts of the group they wanted to benefit from and what parts (chores, for example) they could do without.

In addition to these constructive logical consequences, there are also positive logical consequences. At Monarch, the most obvious example of a positive logical consequence was a kids' ability to earn overnights with their parents by completing the full backpacking expedition in a supportive way with the rest of the group, the logic being that the more responsibilities they took on for the group's success, the more independence they were granted.

In summary, it works much better if you begin by gently guiding the kids' attention towards noticing the *natural consequences* of their choices—both social (how their choices affect others in the group) and environmental (how their choices relate to their wellbeing within the environment). Sometimes it can also be useful to create *logical consequences* that are clearly explained as supportive of the kids' learning (and never as punishment). Logical consequences, whether positive or constructive, fit logically with the choices the students make: "Do well on the expedition and you will earn your time with your family," or, "You left your stuff out last night, so rather than start hiking now and lose it for good (a natural consequence), we'll start our hike once you find it all on your own (a logical consequence)."

It's important to realize, too, that this is not just a matter of words. If you find yourself judging the kids for their weak points or failure to follow the rules, even if you say all the right words, they will likely respond differently to you. Voice tone and body language convey a great deal—whether or not we want it to, or realize it. Even if the consequence is technically a logical one, kids will respond negatively if their experience is that they are being judged and punished, rather than being guided and supported. This will not only make your job as leader difficult, it will detract from the kids' ability to notice and learn from the natural consequences of each choice.

A POST-SCRIPT ABOUT PUNISHMENT

For those interested, I want to say a little bit more about the research on punishment. First let me clarify that by "punishment" I am referring to the introduction of a noxious stimulus (such as yelling, lecturing, or spanking). This is distinct from removing something positive (such as not paying a kid his regular weekly allowance, telling him to go to his room, or removing other privileges) which in operant conditioning is referred to as *negative punishment*, and does work to a degree. However negative punishment works much more effectively if you describe it in a way that can't be interpreted as either "negative" or as "punishment," by reframing it as *positive reinforcement*, which operant conditioning shows to be the most effective. For example: "Mike, lets check in and see whether you're on track to complete all of your responsibilities so that you can earn your allowance this week." (Presupposition: this is within your control and ability to earn your allowance, and I'm here to support you along the way and reward you with an allowance every week that you complete your responsibilities.) This is much more powerful than waiting until the end of the week to say: "Well Mike, you didn't do your responsibilities, so I'm taking away your allowance this week." (Presupposition: you were entitled to an allowance all along for no good reason, but since you didn't do certain things, I'm taking that away from you as punishment.) (See tool 39, "Earning vs. taking away," page 186)

The overwhelming evidence of both behavioral and psychological research shows that punishment by introducing a noxious stimulus such as yelling, lecturing or spanking is ineffective. So why does a large majority of people in the United States still believe that this kind of punishment works with kids?

One reason is that yelling, lecturing, spanking, etc., often does stop negative behavior in the moment (though less so the older and more independent the kid becomes), making it appear that the punishment is working. But this is an illusion. Many psychological studies have since confirmed what B.F. Skinner, one of the most prominent founders of operant conditioning, concluded in 1972: *"A person who has been punished is not thereby simply less inclined to behave in a given way; at best, he learns how to avoid punishment"* (B.F. Skinner, Beyond Freedom and Dignity). So rather than teach a kid not to do a negative behavior (such as swearing or hitting, etc.), punishment at *best* teaches the kid to suppress the swearing or hitting, but only in contexts where a real threat of punishment exists. Where that threat doesn't exist (such as when an authority figure is not present, or too tired or occupied to carry out the threat, or when a kid grows up and no longer answers to those authorities) the negative behavior continues, or may even increase. Punishment also fails to teach the kid anything about what behavior to do *instead*. The irony in this is that punishment often increases the very behaviors it is employed to eradicate, such as lying, sneaking, and hitting when no one is looking. So far we've been talking about Skinner's best case scenario. At *worst*, punishment won't even work in the moment, and may incite a rebellious, violent backlash.

In parenting literature and research, punishment has been increasingly recommended against. Spanking research clearly indicates that not only does spanking not work (other than gaining immediate compliance), it is correlated with a whole host of problems lasting into adulthood. These include: decreased mental health, decreased parental relationship, decreased ability to internalize morals, increased aggression, increased risk of being physically abused, increased anti-social behavior, increased criminal behavior, and increased risk of abusing a child or spouse. *"You cannot punish out these behaviors that you do not want,"* says Kazdin, who served as president of the American Psychological Association in 2008. *"There is no need for corporal punishment based on the research. We are not giving up an effective technique. We are saying this is a horrible thing that does not work."* [*]

There is another important reason why many well-meaning people still believe punishment is an effective teaching tool: it seems to be effective in our experience. Perhaps this is why the practice of spanking kids has endured so long. Much of the apparent success of spanking (and other punishments) is actually due to the law of regression towards the mean. For example, if I have a range of behavior from "being nice" to "being naughty," this range of behavior will form a bell curve. Only occasionally, on a really good or really bad day, will I be exceptionally nice or exceptionally naughty. Most of the time my behaviors will be somewhere in the middle, with the majority of my behaviors being right in the middle (my average, or mean). So whether I have been exceptionally nice, or exceptionally naughty, the odds

---

[*] Brendan L. Smith, "The Case Against Spanking," *Monitor on Psychology* Vol 43, No. 4 (April 2012): page 60. On the web at: http://www.apa.org/monitor/2012/04/spanking.aspx

are that my next behavior will fall somewhere back towards the middle again. Thus if I am spanked or punished for my exceptionally bad behavior, low and behold my next behavior is much better, the spanking appears to cause the improved behavior! Whereas if I am praised for exceptionally good behavior, the odds are that my next behavior won't be quite so exceptionally good, and it appears that positive praise causes worse behavior! When regression towards the mean is accounted for, however, numerous studies show that positive reinforcement works, while punishment, such as spanking, is ineffective and damaging.

While a large majority of people in the United States still believe that punishment is effective, an even larger majority would prefer not to use punishment if they had an alternative that they believed would work. Enter natural and logical consequences, combined with positive reinforcement (See tool 7, "Praise passionately, discipline indifferently," page 85) as well as all the other tools in this book.

6.

Never set a boundary you can't enforce

Depending on how you set boundaries, you will either set yourself up for power control battles or you won't.

Setting boundaries you can't enforce is worse than setting no boundaries at all. So don't tell a kid they can't leave their tent at night unless you are prepared to stand watch and literally make it impossible. It's a subtle thing, for example at Monarch we had a rule that kids be in eyesight and earshot of a field instructor at all times unless in their tents. I present this to the kids as an expectation, not a boundary, and explain that disregarding this expectation has certain natural and logical consequences, such as reduced trust and inability to earn overnights with family. I would lay out this expectation (and the other simple rules of being in the field) with perfect clarity with the kids, explaining the logic behind each rule/expectation:

"We don't have many rules here, and the rules we do have are for everyone's safety and well being. As long as we all follow the few reasonable rules we have here, then we can actually have a pretty good time even if this is the last place you want to be."

"Reasonable!" Josh complained, "Having to stay in eyesight and earshot is *reasonable?*"

"I agree that wouldn't be a reasonable rule on a vacation, but you aren't here on vacation. You're all here because you have work to do to rebuild a relationship with your parents to the point they feel comfortable having you back home. Your parents have work to do too, and I hope they work just as hard as you will. While you're here I'm legally responsible for you, and while I understand how annoying it is for you not to be able to leave eyesight and earshot, that's the only way I can know I'm keeping you safe to the best of my ability. That's why we have that rule, and that's the reason I'm requesting that you stay in eyesight and earshot at all times."

Megan asked, "Why can't I just have a private conversation once in a while? It's not like I want to share my life with the whole world all the time!"

I said, "We're all here to support each other in getting back home where you can make your own choices and have conversations with whoever you want. While you're here, there is no need to have private conversations. If it's not appropriate for everyone in this group to hear, then it doesn't need to be said."

This is very different than telling a kid, "You can't leave your tent at night," or "you can't have a private conversation," which is simply untrue. They can and do leave their tents at night, and even under the closest supervision there will be times when they find opportunities for side conversations. Telling them that they can't isn't going to change that; it will only make them laugh at you when they do it. Making sure they understand the rules, and laying out clear expectations, is different than telling them they can't do something that they clearly *can* do if they decide to.

So I didn't actually set any boundaries at all, in the strict sense of the word. Instead I communicated clearly why I was doing what I was doing (the logic behind the rules and the natural and logical consequences of not following them). It's important to realize that as I did this, my goal was never to get the kid to agree with me. If the kid senses that you're waiting until they agree with you, they'll have the ability to create quite a bit of conflict, because there is nothing you can do to make them agree. (See tool 4, "There is no *need* or *have to*," page 71, and tool 45, "Manipulation," page 202.) I would often acknowledge that they might not agree at all, and then explain the rule/expectation the way it made sense to me. As Virginia Satir said so eloquently, "Peace comes from understanding, not agreement."

Whether or not the kid agreed with me, I would always talk about logical consequences in terms of the benefits to them, (such as for their learning, safety, or the safety of the group). They might disagree with my methods, but they would hear that my logical consequences were sincerely in order to support them the best way I knew how. I never used consequences as a threat; doing that would be a good recipe for getting into a power control battle.

Saying, "If you physically threaten me or another student, I'm going to call the police," comes across as a threat and could easily escalate a kid into testing me. Notice the difference when I include, and focus on, the benefits to the student and the group: "I want to remind you that one of the rules at Monarch is that no one ever threaten another person here. This is very important in order to keep everyone here safe, including you. I also want to remind you that Monarch policy is to file criminal charges if a student ever threatens another student or staff, and I want to remind you of this because I would much prefer not to have the police involved just because of a mistake. I also know that if something's making you angry, clearly something isn't working for you, and I want to make sure things work for you as much as possible. That's my job. So if something isn't working for you, my request is that you bring it directly to me, so we can address the situation together and make sure your needs are being met without you even coming close to threatening anyone. Will that work for you?"

While focusing on the student/group needs, I'm also *personalizing* everything that puts me on the same side as the student: "*I* would much prefer not to have the police involved," "*I* want to make sure things work for you." I'm also being sure to *depersonalize* and keep unemotional anything that could come across as threatening or blaming: "One of the rules at Monarch," is very different than saying "I won't tolerate threats." "Policy is to file criminal charges," is very different than saying, "I will file criminal charges." "If a student ever threatens another student or staff," is very different than saying, "If you ever threaten another student or staff." This depersonalized language allows me to remain on the side of the student, while "Monarch," or "policy," or "the hypothetical student," or "the rule," can be separate from us and safely criticized or examined or cussed out by the student. (See the next tool 7, "Praise passionately, discipline indifferently" page 85.) Talking about logical consequences in a non-threatening way may take a little longer, but taking this extra time on the front end will save a whole lot of trouble later on, and could even end up saving someone's life. In the "Tales" sections you can read other examples of how I worded my expectations of students as requests rather than commands or ultimatums.

In summary, rather than setting boundaries, I had conversations. I was clear about my reasonable expectations and how those expectations benefitted the group, and I was also clear about the natural consequences and when appropriate also the logical consequences that would result from kids not living up to my expectations.

7.

Praise passionately, discipline indifferently

P raise kid's successes with passion and excitement and let your emotions come through to celebrate. However when it comes to discipline, passion is the last thing you want. This fits right in with natural and logical consequences (tool 5, "Natural and logical consequences," page 74). Anger at a kid has nothing to do with logic, and is an attempt to discipline through fear of your anger rather than any learning from the situation itself. Anger only complicates matters by adding an extra layer that distracts from any learning the kid would otherwise gain. So be very sure to discipline indifferently, simply communicating the natural and logical consequences (if they aren't already clearly evident).

Micah nearly punched Derrick in the face, failing only when the snow collapsed beneath him. I got between them right away and asked them in a firm voice to keep at least 12 feet between them at all times until we got back to camp for a Group. In

Group Micah said, "I'm over it, it's no big deal. Derrick just got me pissed off keeping on throwing snowballs at me."

Neither of them had much to say about it, and I wasn't convinced that another eruption wouldn't happen at a later time. I said, "Micah, I'm asking you to continue to stay at least 12 feet away from Derrick, and the same for you, Derrick, for the rest of the day at least. Obviously you both could have used some extra space earlier today, so I'm asking you to do that ahead of time for the rest of the day."

"We don't need it, we're fine," Derrick said.

"I know you both feel fine now, but I don't yet. It's my responsibility to keep you all safe, and when one kid takes a swing at another I take that seriously. Obviously I didn't realize you needed more space earlier today, Micah, so I want to be sure you have that space for a while. I'll drop the 12 feet request once I feel comfortable that neither of you will get triggered again. I'd hate to tell your parents you got in a fight just because you didn't have enough space in the entire Rocky Mountain wilderness!"

8.

Relationship is influence

The only time I ever felt nervous about anyone in my group was when I didn't know them. When I came back on shift and there were three new kids in my group that I hadn't met before, I got an uneasy feeling in my stomach that seemed to say, "Unknown quantity here, beware." I think this is a pretty universal feeling in this kind of social situation. The problem is, many people try to protect themselves by putting up walls or staying distant. If you're the leader, this is the exact opposite of what you want to do.

Whenever there was a new kid, I wouldn't let anything get in my way of getting to know that kid as soon as possible, so I could support them. I was always both friendly and extremely nosey. All business was my business, and I got very good at remembering names the first time I heard them. Usually the new kids were all introduced to incoming field staff during shift exchange, when we hear an update from outgoing staff about how each kid did the last three weeks, but this doesn't count as getting to know them, because the communication is second-hand and one-way. A relationship is one-on-one, and two-way, even if a lot of the two-way is nonverbal. You have to make the effort to become that kid's friend and ally yourself, one-on-one.

There's no right thing to say, just be human and find anything to talk about to start building a connection. Ask the kid about themselves and what they like and care about. Maybe you'll find commonalities, maybe you'll be fascinated by differences. Either way it's a positive connection.

"Hey Tom, how're things going in the new Monarch life?"

"They pretty much suck."

"Yeah. I get that it's not where most kids want to be. What kind of stuff do you do when you're home that you enjoy?"

"Anything that's not this." This is the kind of answer that would put most people off, but don't let it. They are testing you (though not consciously). Be persistent and show that you really want to know about them as a person.

"So Tom, what's one of those things? Do you like any sports?"

There was rarely a kid that wouldn't tell me about themselves. And as soon as I got to know a new kid, my anxiety would leave. Now they were a known quantity, a human being I could work with no matter how difficult. I had begun to establish a relationship, the only means of influence I chose to use. Using any other form of influence, such as force or coercion, would go against the purpose of the program.

A POST-SCRIPT ABOUT FORCE

There is an exception to the general rule of not using force as a means of influence. Physically restraining a kid who is out of control and putting themselves or others in danger can be a positive use of force as influence, *if done properly*. Think of how often babies are physically held back or restrained from getting themselves into trouble. This is needed less and less as a child grows and becomes self sufficient. When considering restraining a teen, the first step is to be trained in how to do it safely. When you are trained, you will know that one of the first things to check is whether the kid is small enough that the physical struggle of the restraining process won't cause more damage than letting them be. If a kid is too strong, a restraint isn't even an option. It is also very important that the restraint be done fully in the interests of the kid (such as preserving their immediate safety and the immediate safety of their group members). If a restraint is used to end a power control battle, or satisfy some power trip of the person/people doing the restraint, it will not only put the kid (and those performing the restraint) under unnecessary physical risk, but also cause emotional damage. If your reasons for restraining are pure, but a kid turns out to be stronger than you thought and your restraint goes wrong, the result can also be increased emotional as well as physical damage. Mostly the kids I worked with were too big to consider a restraint. With the kids that were small enough, I always found other ways through the tools in this book.

9.

Go towards the scary stuff

It's very important to have no topic you are unwilling to bring up and discuss. In the above example I ask Tom about what he likes to do at home, a light topic, but I never stopped there. I showed kids from the get-go that I wasn't afraid of any of their problems. If they saw that I was afraid of their problems, then how could I possibly help them? So very soon I'd ask them why they were sent here. No need to make this a "serious" conversation, just ask about it, and find out whether it's serious or not to the kid.

"So Tom, what brought you here?"

"My stupid parents."

"Why'd they do that?"

"They don't want me to be doing drugs."

"What kind of drugs?"

"Pot, E, heroin, cocaine..." Many people would stop here, or even at Tom's previous answer, filling in their own idea of what "doing drugs" is and moving on, either due to a fear of the conversation topic, inexperience with it, or a judgment along the lines of, "Drugs are bad, end of story," which is a great way to alienate a kid. Remember to go towards the scary stuff. I have very little experience with hard drugs, but that doesn't mean I can't have a conversation about them. In fact these are the best conversations, because I might actually learn something new to me, and that makes it more interesting. Kids will recognize when you're interested in what's important to them.

"So which is your favorite drug?" I asked Tom. That got his attention a little bit. He probably never had an authority figure ask him something like that before.

"The heroin and cocaine, and the E. And the pot too, I guess. All of it. I've done other stuff too."

"What other stuff have you done? What was your best experience of all, and your worst experience of all?"

Kids usually love talking about the scary stuff, because it's some of the most important parts of their lives, whether for good or bad or both. And up until now it's likely they've never had this conversation with an adult before. As the conversation develops, I'm finding out where this person's motivation lies. What are his goals, what does he care about?

"So what does doing drugs get you, that you enjoy so much?"

"Oh man, when I'm on E it's like the past and future drop away and I'm just in the moment, it's awesome."

"That does sound great. I haven't done E, but I've had that kind of experience of being in the moment in the middle of a tough rock climb where I was super focused on every piece of rock I could possibly use as a handhold." Just make sure you don't let yourself be steered away from the "scary" topic and into your own story. "So are you at all worried about what these drugs may be doing to your body over time?" This is not a trick question, I'm actually interested in finding out if Tom sees this as a concern or not.

You get the idea. If something seems like a "scary" topic, focus on that. Take tangents and sidetracks, get lighter and make jokes, but come back and continue to really explore the scary stuff. That's why these kids are here, after all. Show them your genuine interest in their lives, and that none of their problems scare you.

10.

Wait for "contact"

"Fuck you!" Karen yelled at me. "You don't know what you're talking about. You have no respect for me, and you're just out here making money off kids with stupid parents!!"

When I first began working at Monarch, I would have focused on Karen's words, attempting to address everything she said with a logical response. But that doesn't make sense when a kid is pissed off, because they're not in a logical place, they're in an *emotional* place. The words are mostly irrelevant, especially to them, caught up in the emotional moment. So I learned to respond to the emotion with something very simple like this:

"I get that you're really angry right now. Even though you don't believe it, I'm here to support you and I'm happy to talk about your concerns as soon as you can be in contact with me." Contact, again, is the Gestalt Therapy word we used at Monarch to mean not only eye contact, but also communicating truthfully and listening and taking in what someone else is communicating.

"I am fucking in contact!" Karen screamed back at me. "I want to talk about this now, and you don't care about me enough to fucking even talk!"

Here is where it's easy to get hooked back in, to try to give a logical argument to defend your position. But the trick is that your position needs no defense. She's not going to believe a word you say, anyway, and she especially won't if you tell her you'll talk when she's in contact, and then you take her bait and keep talking when she's clearly not. So again I repeated, "I'm here to support you and I'm happy to talk with you whenever you're ready to be in contact. Right now I'm not experiencing contact with you."

"Yes I am in contact, you asshole!"

Sometimes I would agree with such a statement and exaggerate, "*Asshole* is putting it lightly! I'm such a fuck-up I voluntarily *joined* this screwed up hell-hole of a program!" This would often take the wind out of a kid's sails, causing them to laugh or be less angry (See tool 29, "Exaggerate," page 145). Sometimes I would just let a kid vent at me a bit more, to get out their anger. Sometimes I'd tell them that when I'm angry, I like to yell across the valley or break sticks, and they could do that if they liked. But what I wouldn't do was get caught in the arguments and words.

With Karen, I just moved on to something else that needed doing in camp. She could vent and argue as much as she liked, but I didn't have anything more to say until she was ready to really communicate—both talking and listening.

When she saw she couldn't get a rise out of me, she did cool off on her own for a bit. Later when she came back to me with her concerns she acknowledged that she hadn't been in contact. "I'm ready to be in contact now, though," she told me. "Can we talk?"

"Of course."

And she communicated her needs, listened to my responses, and we talked about how we could make life better for her out here. It worked this way for many kids, not just Karen.

11.

Make contact with the kids

Don't accidentally delete yourself from the equation. Just because this isn't about you, doesn't mean that you aren't a human being, with your own needs and wants and emotions. Feel free to share how you feel when other kids do x, y, or z. They want to know and see that you are human, and that you can open up and be vulnerable. That is actually a huge *strength* in your leadership. Remember that you can always ask a kid, "Can I make contact with you?" Or in plain English, "Can I connect with you?" Get permission first, if there's no permission there's no point. If they say no, respect that, and ask if there's another time that works.

Mostly kids said "yes" to me when I asked to be in contact with them. Then I shared with them whatever my experience was, using Nonviolent Communication or other form of "I" language:

"Thanks for listening to me. I just wanted to let you know that when I see you stop caring about group chores, resigning yourself to solo for day after day after day, I feel sad because I want you to have a life you're excited about. I've really enjoyed connecting with you over the weeks, and I think you're a really great girl. So I just wanted to share that I feel sad when I see you no longer a part of the group. I respect your choice in what you want to do, and I want you to know that I'd be really happy to have you back as part of the group again."

12.

Attach the kids to you

Under no circumstances did we ever withhold basic necessities as a means of control or punishment. No matter how much a kid misbehaved, they never went hungry or thirsty or without a dry place to sleep. This is the most basic and most important level of care that anyone can show for another person. If I'm meeting a kid's basic needs, they will notice, even through their hatred of being in the program. They can argue that I'm not there for them, but they will experience that I *am* there for them when it comes to meeting their most important needs.

Often it takes days or weeks or even months for old patterns to wear off and for the kids to realize that you are a different person from the authority figures in their life back home. But once a kid realizes that you will meet their basic needs no matter what they do, they will begin to feel fundamentally accepted as a human being, and will develop a deepening trust of you as someone who meets their needs. This lays the foundation for further trust to be built between you and them regarding other, less basic needs and desires. They have an opportunity to show you that *you* can also trust *them*, and many will work hard to earn your trust in order to gain greater autonomy and freedom beyond simply having their basic needs met.

Often kids at Monarch were never attached healthily to their parents, because from the very beginning, not many of their needs were met by their parents. Duey Freeman, one of the elder therapists at Monarch, taught us about the "attachment cycle," an elegant model he developed to explain why we never want to withhold meeting kids' basic needs as a form of control or punishment. It goes like this:

When kids are babies, they have needs. When they want food they start sucking, when they're uncomfortable, they start squirming, etc. If the mom or dad doesn't figure out what they want, they start crying. Then they cry louder. When the need is met, the baby experiences relief, and this builds trust with the caretaker. Most babies get most of their needs met most of the time. They're hungry, they get fed, they're sleepy, they get lulled to sleep, they need a diaper change, or to be burped, and on and on. Each of these needs that is met by the parent further attaches the child to that parent—hundreds of times per day.

But some babies don't get most of their needs met. Those babies go into a hysterical cry, almost like a rage. Sometimes that works, but when it doesn't, the kid shuts down, just goes still and quiet. It's an eerie thing.

So kids that aren't well attached to their parents learn that rage is their only chance of getting what they want, and often they give up, shut down, and don't even try. So our job as field staff is to re-attach the kids to us—to become their surrogate parents who will provide for them whether they are nice or obnoxious. Once they experience us meeting their basic needs, this builds enough trust that they will start to come to us for help with other needs, such as how to solve more complex problems in their lives.

It's important to remember that part of providing for their basic needs is providing for their safety, and that means boundaries. As Duey also taught us, when kids reach about 2 years old, they start pushing back on parents. When boundaries are set, they might cry or make a fuss, but they *want* to feel those boundaries. They want to feel that there are people looking out for them who are wiser and stronger than they are. When 2-year-olds push, they *want* to feel a safe container holding them in.

The same thing is true of teens, though the container is much larger than with a two-year-old—teens are in the final stage of childhood before becoming independent adults. Teens will push you to see what you're made of, and though consciously they'll be angry and disappointed by the lack of freedom, they'll feel safe when they feel those appropriate boundaries. When the teen is ready to no longer have those final boundaries, they will be ready to become their own caretaker as an independent adult.

Because teenagers are in the process of becoming independent adults, I often had a group conversation to discover how everyone would like the group to operate. It's amazing how often the kids come up with exactly the same rules that you would have otherwise had a whole lot of trouble convincing them to follow!

Group Dynamics

13.

Positive peer pressure

You become the leader of a group when a majority recognizes that you will be the best at meeting their needs. If you can show them this, the group will gladly follow your lead. I often used positive peer pressure to get results instead of trying to do it all myself.

"Would anyone like to share how they felt when Jessica started cussing at Sarah?" I asked during a Group.

"Yeah, I'll share," Morgan said. "It really got me down, even though it wasn't directed at me. We're all going through tough times, so we should all be supporting each other."

Using positive peer pressure both established me as a leader who was including everyone's needs, and also helped the kids learn better social skills. I frequently used positive peer pressure to guide wayward kids into the fold. Students often could care less what I thought, but they rarely did anything to lower their status in the group. If the culture of a group had been established in a clear and positive way, with me as their accepted leader, then one or two new kids had a very hard time disrupting that.

This is also the reason we had incoming students start with a day or two of solo time, staying separate from the group in their tents while they read about our group rules that served to keep everyone safe and happy in the woods. Solo time gave incoming kids a chance to process what just happened, whether they knew ahead of time that they were coming to a wilderness therapy program, or simply found themselves "kidnapped" from their bedrooms one morning and brought into the field. Solo time gave them a chance to get a little distance between them and home, and time to genuinely look forward to the positives of joining the group, as opposed to resenting it. Before joining the group, incoming students were also required to complete several written assignments regarding rules and expectations, and how to live with comfort and safety in the wilderness setting. All of this ensured that new kids were usually relatively happy to join the group and already understood the rules and expectations for how to be a supportive team member. If they didn't show an understanding of the rules and expectations (or the ability to learn them quickly), I was always happy to put them back on solo for some more studying until they could show me and the rest of the group that they were ready to be a positive addition to the group.

14.

Align the group with you

Sometimes I asked a kid to go on solo and he or she refused to move away or refrain from talking with the rest of the kids. In such a case I would call a Group right away, and be sure to align the rest of the group with me, again through natural and logical consequences. When Kevin refused to go on solo I called a Group and said:

"Kevin is on solo for not participating in the group chores that you all need done to have a good time out here. I've asked Kevin to go on solo until he's ready to return to the group, but so far he is refusing. I apologize to the rest of you who have to put up with this, and I ask that you honor his solo by not talking to Kevin even though he's breaking solo by talking to you. Because he's choosing to not be part of the group, and he's breaking solo, so far he isn't earning any family nights at the end of the expedition.

"I know that Kevin's behavior makes it harder for all of you, but as long as the rest of you honor his solo by not inter-acting with him, and work together as a group, the rest of you have full opportunity to earn all your family nights when we finish this expedition. While Kevin chooses not to be a full member of the group, it's important that we keep it clear that we're glad to let him be a part of the group as soon as he's ready to be a full member of the group, which means pulling his weight just like the rest of you are doing. Until then, I ask that you don't talk to Kevin even if he talks to you. Is everyone willing to do this?"

Here I'm watching the group for not only verbal agreement, but much more important, nonverbal agreement. If I get that, then I still ask, "Does anyone have any concerns about this?" Again, this is not a rhetorical question; I want to hear about any objections up front, so we can take care of them. This is much easier than having objections bubble up later after hours of quiet internal escalation.

"Yeah, I have a concern," Ross said. "It's not fair for Kevin to be able to say whatever he wants to any of us and we can't even say anything back."

"Thanks Ross, I agree it's certainly not an ideal situation. If you could say stuff back to Kevin, what would that get you that's important?"

"Well then I'd be able to defend myself if he says something crazy about me."

"OK, so its important to you to be able to defend yourself if Kevin says something untrue or crazy about you."

"Yeah!"

"Great, I think that's important too. Can you or the group think of ways that you can defend yourself without engaging with Kevin? Maybe it would be to agree as a group that as long as Kevin isn't participating with and contributing to the group, no one in the group will put any weight in the things Kevin says about any of you. Would that work?"

"Well," Ross said, "I guess if the whole group agreed to ignore the crazy things he says about me, then I wouldn't need to talk back to Kevin. We could all just ignore him as long as we *all* agree that nothing he says about us is worth listening to."

"OK, great. This makes sense to me. Does everyone in the group agree to this?" I waited to get clear nods or "yeses" from everyone before proceeding: "And Ross, if you still find yourself wanting to talk back or defend yourself after something that Kevin says, can you come to me instead? Then I can defend you and make sure you get your needs met without you having to engage with Kevin? Will that work for you, because I want to do everything I can to make sure that the group members who are doing well are also treated well."

"Yeah, I can do that."

"Thank you. I really appreciate all of you agreeing to this. I know it's not easy when a group-member refuses to cooperate. It makes it harder for everyone in the group; I won't forget that. Is there anything else that anyone in the group needs to feel good about this plan of not engaging with Kevin, and coming to me first if you have a need that isn't being met?"

Everyone shook their heads.

As much as possible, I did my best to address any concerns or objections right away, so we would be a strong and united group regardless of a single kid trying to meet his needs through actions that negatively affected the group.

15.

Group

I almost never let a schedule interfere with group process, unless the schedule had to do with safety. This was a great way of solving problems before they became problems, and a great example of "going towards the scary stuff," (tool 9, "Go towards the scary stuff," page 90) or in this case, "going towards the stuff that might turn scary if it's not recognized and addressed head on."

Mostly the kids didn't like having a Group unless there was really something important to talk about and resolve. Kids don't want to waste their time talking just for talking's sake; there are plenty of more fun things to be doing. So if kids were bickering or getting on each other's nerves, I always found it useful to suggest that we have a Group about it. It showed that I was taking them seriously by making their concerns important enough to suggest a formal Group. It validated their concerns and showed that I valued their feelings. If there really was something important to talk through and figure out, then we'd have a Group and get a lot out of it. But often it really wasn't that big of a deal, so the kids would say something like, "No, no, that's OK, we don't really need a whole Group about it." If, later on, the same bickering surfaced, I'd simply have to say, "Do you guys want to have a Group?" Usually they'd quit the bickering, having publicly agreed it wasn't worth wasting time on a Group. But if not we'd simply have the Group. Either way it was a win.

Now imagine if, instead of taking their bickering seriously, I'd said something like, "C'mon, just drop it, this isn't that big of a deal." First, I'd risk missing something that really *was* important to someone, even if it didn't seem important to me. Second, even if I was right and it wasn't a big deal, my failure to acknowledge their *possible* needs *is* a big deal, which will often compel kids to turn something that isn't a big deal into something that is. Now it's not about the bickering anymore, it's about whether or not you show that you're caring and supportive. Failing to acknowledge a small problem or annoyance early can allow it to escalate over time into a big problem. A little bickering over five or ten minutes is one thing, but if it continues unaddressed for days, that can poison the whole culture of a group, and become a habit that is tough to change.

Once I was driving my group back from Arizona to Colorado after our backpacking expedition, and the kids were starting to get on each other's nerves. "Hey guys," I said, "I know it's a long drive, and we all wish we were back out hiking in the snow instead of cramped in a warm van, but that's life for you. Shall we stop and have a Group about what's going on back there?"

"No, please," Gavin said, "We're almost home. I want to get some sleep before seeing my parents tomorrow."

"Yeah, we can be cool," Steve said. "We can be cool, right guys? I'm in the middle of telling a story. Trust me, you guys will want to hear the end of this."

"Does everyone feel the same way? That you'd rather not have a group right now?" I made sure I saw a nod in the rear-view mirror, or heard a verbal response, from each of the kids. "Well as long as I hear you all getting along, I'm happy if you're

happy," I said. "I just want to make sure you're all as ha
possible, given the cramped nature of van rides."

Ten minutes later, when some bickering started up ag
said, "So is it time for a Group after all?"

"No, no! Guys, come on! Do you want to get back home, or
spend another hour in a group on the side of the road?"

"Yeah, we can do this. It's only a couple more hours." The
kids got themselves under control and we had a good ride the
rest of the way back to Colorado. Other times I did stop the van
and have a Group on the side of the road, but only once or twice.

Of course if I saw some form of bullying—a problem experienced by one kid, and not the others, then *I* held a Group
because *I* wanted to hold a Group. I don't tolerate mistreatment
of anyone in my group, even at a subtle level. Here's where it's
very important to not leave the decision to hold a Group up to
the group. And it's just as important not to leave the decision
up to the victim, who might be further victimized by "wasting
everyone's time with another Group." (For more on this see tool
24, "Bullying: (Standing up for the underdog)," page 131.)

16.

"Contact" in groups

"When George goes on about how bad the army is, it pisses me off, 'cause my Dad was in the Marines!"

"OK, Michael," I said, "Can you look at George and tell him directly?"

"Yeah, George, it really pisses me off when you bad-mouth the US army."

"OK, thanks Michael," I said, "George, would you like to respond to Michael?"

George looked at me, "Hey, I have nothing against Michael's Dad, I just don't like the army and what it does."

"Can you look at Michael and tell him that directly?" I ask again.

"He already heard it."

"Yeah, I heard him," Michael said. "He hates our troops."

"I know you heard him, Michael," I said. "George, I'd still like you to express whatever you want to express directly with Michael. Because this is really between you two, and it's important to be able to make contact and look each other in the eye even when we disagree, because everyone in this group is going to disagree at times.

"All right," George said, looking at Michael, softening a bit. "Michael, I've got nothing against your dad, I just don't like what the army does in general."

"OK. I hear you," Michael said, softening a bit as well. "But we're in big disagreement on that one."

It's important to keep reminding kids to speak to each other directly, while coaching them as much as possible to speak of their own experience and to leave judgment of others out of it. When they speak through you, they don't yet know how to speak directly to the other person, or they're rightly cautious that the other person might get upset. With you there as guide, you can give them the direct instructions so they begin to learn how to do it themselves. I never robbed the kids of this valuable learning experience by speaking for them.

Once one kid has communicated his or her own experience directly, with eye contact, then invite whoever is receiving the communication to share, if he or she wishes, how they feel hearing the direct communication.

If a kid doesn't seem able to express himself, you might step into his shoes and say, "Sally, if I were in your situation, I'd feel _____. Is that true for you at all, or do you feel differently?"

At other times, a kid may not be in a place where they're ready to *receive* feedback. When I had feedback for a kid who I sensed might not be open to hearing it, I asked a simple question: "Sam, I have some feedback that I think could help you, would you like to hear what it is?" I almost never got a "no" to this question, because now Sam gets a bit curious, and feels respected because I asked for his permission. "Yeah, sure," Sam says. "Thanks, Sam, I just noticed that..." Now that Sam has given me permission, he has a new openness to listen and take in feedback that he might have otherwise found threatening. So in a group facilitation, I often said, "Henry, are you open to hearing some feedback from David right now?" If the answer was "no," then I would ask Henry, "When is a time you're open to making contact with David and hearing from him?" If the answer was "never" (which it rarely was), then I would ask Henry to be on solo until he decided he was ready to be a full participating member of the group.

17.

Lead by giving over leadership/ responsibility

"Leader of the Day" was the single most useful tool for me while leading Monarch groups. Each day on expedition, I would choose a new student to be the leader of the day, or LOD. I told them that the job of the leader of the day is to look out for the interests of the group for that day. I would confer with them and show them the map, and what kind of hike we had ahead of us. The leader would be in charge of pacing, water breaks, etc. The leader was also encouraged to take a more active part in Groups, making sure every voice was heard, etc. Then, at the end of the day, the group would give feedback on what they liked about how the LOD had led the day, and what they thought could be improved. I would always ask that each improvement be given in a positive way, "Here is what I wish you had done" followed by a clear example. After the group feedback, I would give my own feedback—again with positive examples of what I thought would work even better.

The Leader of the Day tool accomplished so much all at once:

First, it gave a good way of interfacing with the group (another form of positive peer pressure), taking pressure off me and allowing the group to take more responsibility and owner-ship of their own experience. When someone asked how long the hike was, I'd say, "I don't know, better ask the leader of the day." When I thought it was a good idea to have a water break, I'd suggest it to the LOD and let them tell the group. The group tended to respect the leader of the day, knowing that one day soon they would find themselves in that position.

Second, when students are put in a leadership position, they not only become more self-sufficient, but they also start to appreciate how tough a job it is to look out for the interests of the whole group and balance everyone's needs. By giving them this little bit of authority and responsibility, they become much more grateful that you are doing it most of the time, and that you have ultimate authority if anything gets beyond their ability to handle.

Third, Leader of the Day is versatile. For students who don't want to be leader, it is a great growth opportunity. For students who *want* to be leader, they must implicitly accept your author-ity in order to gain their own for the day. Either way it's a posi-tive outcome both for your leadership of the group, and for the lessons learned by each group member.

18.

Better to start off too tight and loosen up, than to start off too loose and then try to tighten up

This principle was no more clearly demonstrated than on the trip from hell, as I like to call it. When I came into the field to take over the group, I learned that the previous expedition leaders had completely lost control of the group. Both field instructors were pretty new, and for one of them it was her first time leading a group in the field. I don't remember the full details, but it ended up with the rookie leader afraid for her safety, running away into the woods to escape the kids—not a good situation. The cops were called, and nothing horrible happened.

But when I took over the group, it became increasingly clear that these leaders—out of their depth—had let many of the basic rules and expectations slide. Now my co-instructor and I were stuck with the job of tightening back up again, and of all the crazy things that happened to me in this job, this was the toughest expedition I led. I got resistance at every turn. It also didn't help that everyone came down with the flu after our first night.

"Pierce, stay in eyesight and earshot at all times." "Taylor, you need to OK your tent site with me first." "Brandon, no private conversations." "Jordan, remember to wash your hands after using the latrine." My days were a constant stream of nagging and reminding on basic rules that ordinarily went unquestioned, but this group challenged constantly. It was worse than starting with an entirely new group of kids, because this group had a *negative* culture. Every chance he got, Pierce would slowly drift away from the group to see if I would call him back when he started to disappear in the trees. Taylor would not only make decisions without my OK, he would actively defy me and cuss me and other students out when he didn't get his way. Brandon complained as if some great injustice had occurred when I confiscated his "journal entry," which was in fact a long personal note he wrote to one of the girls in our group.

The whole structure usually taken for granted—the positive group culture—had been lost on the previous expedition. Now my co-instructor Jess and I had to slowly build it back again by showing, each tiny step of the way, that we would not allow the total chaos of the previous three weeks.

This also shows the importance, not only of being on the same page with your co-instructor, but also everyone else in charge of the same group of kids. Thankfully, most of the time the group culture was well established and the staff strictly upheld the rules. When this is the established norm, then it's easy to loosen up on certain areas that aren't relevant with a high-functioning and trustworthy group. The students appreciate this demonstration of trust, and I was sure to let them know that any loosening up was because they earned it.

Of course, I always followed policy, and rarely was there any reason to change the basic rules of the group. But let's say a new kid is a run risk, so I'd have him count or sing a song whenever he went to the bathroom out of eyesight. After getting to know him, if I judged him to no longer be a risk, I might not require him to sing while peeing. If kids didn't have my trust, I did my best to be right in the middle of every conversation they ever had. For more trustworthy kids, I'd feel OK allowing them a little more latitude. As long as they demonstrated to me that they didn't need such a tight leash, I was happy to let them have more ownership and freedom.

19.

Structure

A group loves and appreciates the safety that comes of good rituals and habits (i.e. structure). Life is confusing if you're constantly wondering how to act and behave. So as a leader, if you just tell your group what the structure is, they will be grateful for it. A good rule of thumb is that a group will want 80-90% ritual (or habit), and 10-20% novelty.

Whether you are leading a group in the wilderness, leading a class, or leading your own kids in your home, it's very important to think about what kind of structure will work well to support everyone's needs (and of course the structure for various groups will vary depending on the composition and purpose of the group). Some of the structures in place at Monarch—the rules and rituals listed below—will be specific to Wilderness Therapy. Many others may at first appear unique to the setting of a wilderness program, but upon further thought there are effective ways to modify them and have the same basic structure work to support you in the classroom with your students, or the living room with your kids.

For example "solo" time can be utilized very effectively in a classroom or living room setting. All you need is another room, or a back corner of the same room. And what would it be like to have a "leader of the day" in the classroom that rotates through the group, giving your students more ownership over the learning process? What about a "leader of the day" that rotates through your kids during a family vacation or other trip? Whether you are a teacher in a classroom or a leader of some other kind of youth group, how could you set up a positive group culture by having an intake structure that makes things easy for you? Such as having students complete certain assignments or reading material about the purpose of the group before having the privilege of becoming part of it?

When you take a look at the structures in place in your particular environment, you may find that some of them work great, while others may actually be working against you, making your job more difficult than it needs to be. You may also notice a lack of structure in areas that could really benefit from it. I hope you are inspired to take the time to experiment with structures that will support you in your unique environment with teens. Having the right structures in place can make all the difference between experiencing your job as a nightmare, or as a sustainable and rewarding pursuit.

Following are the structures that were in place for Monarch groups—the field rules and field rituals:

MONARCH FIELD RULES

1. Students are not allowed to have hands on each other unless it is a part of a sanctioned group activity (such as a low ropes course challenge) or they have been given permission by staff.
2. No private conversations between students (unless by permission of a therapist).
3. If a student threatens a staff or student in any way, either verbally or with something that could be used as a weapon,

criminal charges will be filed. (Sometimes we opted not to file criminal charges if we were satisfied with a resolution of the problem, but it was useful for the students to know that we took this very seriously, and were always fully prepared to file criminal charges).

4. Cooking/Eating:
   a. Hands are to be washed prior to every meal and prior to cooking.
   b. Cooking circles are to be set up in the kitchen. Only two people (one staff, one student) are allowed in the cooking circle. The circle must be made of a physical object (rope, twigs, line in the snow, etc.) so that it is obvious.
   c. Staff must directly supervise stoves when they are lit.
   d. Students are not permitted to have access to fuel unless cooking and directly supervised by staff.
   e. Students, other than the one cooking, must be in their tents or within touching distance of their tents, while meals are being cooked.
   f. Prior to eating, the group will be called together into a designated eating area, the cook will serve each student and a moment of silence will be observed.
   g. Food is served outside of the cooking circle, and students must eat away from the cooking circle.
   h. Dishes are to be sterilized at the end of each day. Sterilizing is done by boiling a pot of water and putting all dishes in it.
   i. After meals mugs must be washed, with their lids screwed on, and either under a tent fly or hung in a tree.
   j. Teeth should be brushed at night after the evening meal.
5. Camp is to be storm-proofed at all times after it is set up, ready for any weather. The kitchen needs to be storm-proofed following all meals.
6. When the group arrives at a campsite, staff assigns chores and tells students where tents should be set up.

7. Camp must be fully set up after arriving, and prior to moving on to the next activity.

8. On days when camp is being moved, camp must be broken down within 45 minutes.

9. There is not any lending, sharing, or borrowing. (Read more about the reason for this rule in tool 47, "Keep Relationships Clean," page 211.)

10. No gum is allowed, due to the difficulty of disposing of it.

11. Field baths are to happen once every 3 days.

12. Students must be in eyesight and earshot at all times, unless they are on solo, at a latrine or in their tents.

13. Students are not allowed to smoke.

14. Students are not allowed to carry lighters, flashlights or knives, except temporarily and under the direct supervision of staff.

15. Students are not allowed to eat any wild foods from the backcountry. The risk of misidentification is not worth it. You may teach them and help them identify these items, but clarify that they are not allowed to taste any, and warn them about the risks of deadly foods, etc.

16. Profanity is strongly discouraged and is to be addressed if it becomes regular/daily.

17. Students must ask permission to go anywhere.

18. Students are not allowed to talk with each other during tent or solo time.

19. One foot must be on the ground at all times unless it is a part of a structured and staff supervised activity such as rock climbing or rafting. This rule is in place to prevent accidents due to climbing or other more dangerous activities that could cause injuries that are difficult to deal with in the wilderness.

20. There should only be one person out of the camp at one time (e.g. the latrine).

21. Camp shoes are to be worn in camp only, not on hikes.

22. Students are not allowed to use open-toed shoes as camp shoes.

MONARCH FIELD RITUALS

- Each incoming kid will go through a period of solo time with their tent set up out of contact from the rest of the group. During this time the student will read all material about program rules and expectations, and do several assignments showing he or she has understood the rules and expectations and is ready to join the group and be a positive contributing member.

- There will be a Group (the entire group gathers in a circle to connect) every day to air any issues anyone has with how the group is functioning.

- There will be a one-page journal assignment each day on a topic of the field-instructor's choice (these journals are later given to the kids' individual therapists).

- Leader of the Day: One student from the group is the point person each day to lead the hike, breaks, and basic flow of the day. At the end of the day, the leader of the day receives feedback from peers on how they did—what was appreciated, and areas of improvement (see tool 17, "Lead by giving over leadership/responsibility," page 111).

- There will be solo time each day for kids to get personal space, journal, read, sleep, whatever. Just no talking and separated, either in or within touching distance of their tents. (Also listed as a field rule during dinner preparation).

- Before the group eats dinner, a moment of silence will be observed, to pray to your gods or lack thereof. (Also listed as a field rule).

- Nightly check-in: After teeth are brushed, there will be a quick nightly check-in with the group in a circle. Everyone might share a high and a low from the day, their most embarrassing moment, or something that no one would guess about them. The possibilities are endless depending on what best fits the group's needs that night—reflection, humor, future aspiration, etc.

20.

Control the rhythms of the group, and you control the group

As described in the previous tool, rituals—whether a moment of silence before a meal or a group check-in before bed—help create a comforting sense of structure, familiarity, and security for both teens and staff. This is especially important in any new situation, whether it be a new class, a new peer group, or a first trip out in the unfamiliar wilderness. When you are the one leading these group rituals, starting and stopping them or guiding from one to the next, you have great influence over the group. Group members become used to you leading them through the rhythms of the day, from one way of being (rowdy and telling jokes along the trail) to another way of being (respectful and listening during a group circle). After days of this they look to you for guidance of how to be, whether or not they realize it.

It's important to switch the rhythms from time to time, to satisfy the need for 10-20% novelty. You can hike at night by the full moon and sleep during the day, have a Group in the middle of the day instead of in the evening, have breakfast a mile down the trail instead of before you start the hike. When they have become used to following your lead, they will follow you out of an old habit, and into something new. This becomes a great unconscious metaphor for how they can become more flexible in life in general, and leave old habits behind if they are no longer useful.

21.

Riddles and group games

There are lots of places on the web where you can find five-minute mysteries, riddles, and simple group games. Entertainment is a key to a happy group.

I would often bring a hacky-sack, or my guitar, or exhaust countless hours telling riddles and five-minute mysteries. "What gets bigger when you take away from it and smaller when you add to it?" I once asked a group of kids as I oversaw them digging the hole for the latrine. The main digger took another shovel full of dirt and tossed it out of the hole, a look of perplexity on his face. It was absolutely hilarious watching the kids struggle with the riddle while they were busy creating the answer right there in the ground in front of them!

Sometimes I would auction off bits of coveted food to the person who most accurately guessed my trivia questions: "What percentage of the US federal budget goes to war?" "How many parts of my dad's body is he missing, and what are they?" "What's the only city built on two different continents?" We had great fun with this.

We'd play ghost, the add-on spelling game, where we go around the circle with each person adding a letter to spell an un-spoken word, until someone challenged. If the challenged person couldn't spell an actual word, then they got a letter "G," while if they *could* spell a word, the challenger got the "G". Whenever someone got G-H-O-S-T, they were eliminated.

We would also play other word games, such as choosing a common word (like "rain" or "love") and going around the circle seeing how many different songs we could come up with containing that word.

There were also physical games that didn't require an item like a soccer ball or a Frisbee. Again, there are tons of these games searchable on the internet. "Bipitty-Bipitty-Bop," is a game where one person stands in the middle of the circle and passes focus around the circle with different "moves" available, trying to get someone to "mess up" and became the next person in the middle. "Attacker defender," is a game that involves running around chaotically based on two simple rules. There were also mind games like "Mafia," a game of lies and deceit that was perfect for playing with a group sitting around a campfire.

We also got playful with our nightly "check-ins." Sometimes, in addition to sharing a "rose" and a "thorn" from the day, we'd also finish by sharing our favorite facial hair, or what our super-power would be if we could choose anything. I would invite group members to come up with ideas and it became a coveted honor to be able to decide upon the creative group check-in question of the day.

Of course you can also just make up games specific to your situation. Once we were in camp on a pile of old mine tailings, so we had lots of little rocks and an old rusty sign up on a dead tree fifty feet away. We spent a good hour seeing how many hits we could get on that sign, and it made a very satisfying sound when a missile struck home. Pretty much everything can become a fun game.

"Last one up off your butt is the one to lead the hike until next break!" I proclaimed to one group that had certain members who were having a hard time getting going after breaks. After that they would jump up so as not to be last and have to go first. These "lesson games" are tailored to the group situation. These kinds of early, fun interventions can be key to preventing tensions from escalating between group members and becoming major problems later on down the line. "First one to finish their group chore gets to decide on the toothbrush song!"

"What's the toothbrush song?"

"It's the song we all attempt to sing together while brushing our teeth tonight!"

22.

You can tell a lot about a group from how they hike

How a group hikes is often how they function together. The leaders will tend to plow ahead, wanting to get to camp. The followers will bring up the rear. The more social kids will clump in the middle side-by-side no matter how often you tell them to stay single file on the trail for low-impact on the alpine environment. Then there are the more wayward creative types that will be all over the place, cutting the trail to find a better way up, or crashing off into the brush to investigate something of interest. These are the ones you want to make sure find their way back after a trip to the bushes to go pee.

You can use how the kids hike as a great teaching/therapeutic tool, because often people's strengths are also their weaknesses. I would often have a day where I asked all the hikers up front to hike behind the group, and all those who hiked behind to hike in front. Everyone would complain, but the results were always interesting. For example, the slow kids hated being in front, because then they felt they were holding up the group; they had that visceral pressure of knowing everyone was behind them. Of course we had to go at the slowest person's pace no matter where they hiked in the group, but even so the slow kids always put up huge resistance to walking in front. Similarly, the fast kids really hated going in back. They preferred to run up ahead, wait while the slow kids caught up, then hike really fast again.

But when I had them switch places for the day, the fast kids quickly saw that everyone got into camp faster when the slow kids set the pace. The fast kids came to realize that by leading from behind, they could get their goal faster.

The lesson for the slow kids was usually harder for them to see, because they were the ones really struggling with the hike already, but the lesson for them was no less important: *being slower or less strong doesn't mean you have less right to ask for breaks compared to the fast kids.* When I put the slow kids in front, I told them they could go whatever pace they wanted, as long as they kept moving, and they could take short breaks whenever they needed them. I reminded them that the whole group had to stick together regardless, so this would make it easier for us all to stay together as a group, and to ensure that they got just as much break time as the fast kids. The lesson for the slow kids was also in not letting them ignore their effect on the group by hiding in the back. But of course it's important that this be done in a very positive, acknowledging way:

"We're all one group here," I said to them, "And I'm not OK with you getting left at the back all the time. As soon as you catch up with the front of the group, they're already rested and they start up again, and you don't even get a chance to rest. By having you up front, we can all have equally long breaks and all stay together on the hike. It's OK that you hike slower, some of us are stronger than others. So for the stronger hikers, it's important to stick with the group and support those of us for whom it's a bigger struggle. As long as we keep moving we'll get to camp at any pace." I learned that keeping moving was the key. No matter how slow your hikers are, if they keep moving, you'll reach camp before nightfall. If, on the other hand, you have slow hikers and each break stretches beyond 3 to 5 minutes, to more like 10, 15 or 20 minutes, then you might be in trouble. It's not the hiking pace, but the break length that matters, because on breaks you're going nowhere.

There was always huge resistance from the slow hikers to hike in front, but once they did, no one in the group could ignore anyone else. Letting kids hike in their own natural pattern will tell you a lot about how the group is currently functioning, and that will tell you how you can switch the group hiking order to literally bring the group closer together.

23.

Take charge

Taking charge is hugely important, so learn to have a loud voice that demands attention. Most things are just a matter of simple logistics, and the kids aren't going to put up any resistance to you. They want a leader who knows he (or she) is in charge and who takes charge and gets the group moving in a positive way.

When a big group is milling around, and someone needs to get their attention, I've noticed that most people won't speak loudly enough to get everyone's attention. If you're the leader, this shows that you're letting the group take charge, and you're waiting for when the group is ready. A lot of people don't want to raise their voice because it feels like shouting, it feels negative, or it just feels different and uncomfortable. Learn to raise your voice, because it's a simple matter of physics. If a group of 8-12 kids is all talking or engaged in various different activities, you'll need to raise your voice simply to get them to hear you. Better to do it loudly and clearly the first time, rather than tentatively and wait around for them to notice you. It will tell a very different tale about what kind of a leader you are.

"ALRIGHT EVERYONE, LISTEN UP!" I'd boom. Most people would hear me, but if a few didn't, I'd call their individual names, "Jason, Miles! Everyone listen up please!" I'd wait until I had everyone's attention before going on. If I didn't wait for full attention, that would teach that they don't *really* need to listen up when I ask. Often I would wait and watch the two kids still talking until the rest of the group would tell them to be quiet and listen up so we could get on with it!

24.

Bullying:
(Stand up for the underdog)

One of the most supportive things you can do with your power as a leader and role-model with teens, is to stand up for the underdog. If there is a conflict between two kids who are relatively equal in terms of the power they each hold in the group, then you can support them both in getting to their outcomes and finding solutions that meet both of their outcomes. But if one kid is clearly the underdog, with much less power/status, then as the leader of the group (the top dog) you may need to give much more of your power toward supporting the underdog to create an even relationship where both kids can get their needs met. The underdog needs enough support to eventually feel safe in truly expressing his or her needs. I was always sure to demonstrate to underdogs that they had my support more than anyone else in the group.

In the documentary film "Bully" there are lots of examples of this *not* happing. In one, a teacher tells a victim of bullying to shake hands with the bully (as if this would somehow solve the bullying issue). Understandably, the kid didn't want to shake hands with his bully, to which the teacher responded by blaming the victim for not being willing to "shake hands and make things right." Obviously this teacher had no idea how to deal with bullying, and inadvertently sided with the bully—the one with all the power—giving absolutely no support whatsoever to the underdog.

Once I was in a group where the three "popular" kids in the group started poking fun and laughing at a new boy who had recently joined. The new boy, Jordy, was socially awkward, with long scraggly hair that often got caught in his mouth. "I think Jordy's gonna get a hairball soon," Devon taunted. "Hey, Jordy, have you ever had a hairball?" Jim and Justin called up to where Jordy was hiking. Jordy just shook his head and took it, continuing to hike with his head downcast.

"Everyone stop," I said. "Everyone group up for a moment please."

"Justin, Jim, Devon," I said, waiting until I had each of their eye contact, "I know you guys are just wanting to play around, and I like that, playing around is great. At the same time, if I was Jordy, having just come into a new group and not knowing you guys yet, I wouldn't like having hairball jokes made about me. Those are the kinds of jokes that are only fun for me when I know I have a solid friendship with someone. So if you guys want to make that kind of joke, I ask that you keep such jokes about the three of you until you have as clear a friendship with Jordy as you have with each other."

"It was all in good fun," Justin said. "I think Jordy knows that, don't you Jordy?"

Jordy looked up and jerked his head in a nod.

"We didn't mean anything by it," Devon said.

"Yeah," Jim added, "We're all friends here. Jordy, you're cool with us joking around with you, right?"

"Yeah, I guess," Jordy said, looking at the ground.

"See, he says he's cool with it," Jim said.

Clearly Jordy was in such a weak position, such an underdog, that he didn't even feel comfortable communicating his
reluctance to agree with them. So I wasn't going to ask him to
share his point of view, which was clearly impossible for him at
this point. Instead I was going to show him that I would stand
up for him in a situation where he couldn't stand up for himself. I would only invite him to share his point of view later in
the expedition once he knew—based on his own experience—
that I'd be there for him 100%. But I'd wait to do this until I
was pretty sure he felt supported enough to be able to share his
experience truthfully.

I looked at Jim, "That's fine, Jim. I'm still not cool with any
joking about Jordy. I've led a lot of groups, and my experience is
that even when things are meant in good fun, it's important to
develop clear friendships first. Just as you and Devon and Justin
have become good friends, supporting each other and helping
each other out with packs and setting up tents and stuff, you
guys can do that for Jordy too. If the three of you want to joke,
fine, I ask that you keep it among the three of you."

They agreed, but during our lunch break a few hours later,
Jim started acting like a cat, imitating the way Jordy licked tuna
fish grease off his fingers after the meal. "Jordy, did you have
cats for parents?" Devon added. "Were you sent here by cats?"

If I had let this slide, then Jordy would know that I wasn't
really willing to support him when tested, and Jordy's basic need
for social acceptance would not get met. "Time for a Group," I
said. Earlier I had set my boundary around not making jokes
about Jordy, and every boundary I set I was prepared to keep,
(tool 6, "Never set a boundary you can't enforce," page 81) or
redefine (tool 3, "Power control battles," page 64). When we
were circled up, I said, "Jim, Devon. It's important to me that
when you make an agreement with me, in this case not joking
about Jordy, that you honor that agreement. What do you guys
need, so that it will be easy for you to honor the agreement?"
Again, I'm framing this in their interests (tool 2, "Frame everything in their interests," page 62).

"It just slipped out," Devon said, "sort of how we joke with each other all the time."

"What do you need so that it won't slip out in the future?"

"Maybe to just let us joke around and have some fun, and not be so uptight about it."

"I'm happy to have you joke around about each other, between the three of you. If you're having trouble coming up with things about the three of you, we could have a group brain-storm about it," I said with a smile.

"Whatever, if you want to make this awful place even worse!"

"I want to make this group as supportive and positive as possible. In general we have a rule of not making jokes about anyone in the group, but since the three of you guys are such good friends, I'm happy if you want to make jokes just about each other. But if it's too much of a problem to keep jokes just about the three of you, we can go back to just having no jokes. Would anyone else in the group like to share your experience about this?"

"Yeah," Another student spoke up. "I think it's best in gen-eral not to joke about each other. Even if it's meant in good fun, it can be misinterpreted, and get the whole group down and negative. I think the group was the most positive when there weren't any jokes about anyone."

After this meeting, things improved, but if they hadn't, my next step with any kids who still couldn't control themselves from making jokes about Jordy, would have been to put them on solo. In that event I would have framed it in his interest like this, "Devon, I'm going to ask you to go on solo to make it really easy for you not to slip up and make accidental jokes about others." (See also Chapter Three, "The Trip from the Hall of Fame," for an example of me joining with the underdog in a conflict where one kid threatened another.)

When you stand up for the underdog, you are not only sup-porting the weakest kid, but also being the best possible role model for the kids in the group with the most social power. A positive leader is one who uses his/her social power and status to look out for everyone in the group, and make sure *everyone* stays safe and provided for, regardless of status and social station (which can and does change over time). A negative leader is one who only rewards and looks out for those in the group in relative proportion to the status those individuals already have. This is a weak leader, barely clinging to power through showing favor and alliance only to the others with the most power. This creates an environment that benefits no one, where anyone is at risk of falling lower in status, and having fewer needs met.

In a group with a positive leader, the individual in the position of lowest status gets their basic needs met just as completely as those in the positions of highest status. Everyone is happier, knowing all will be cared for, and thus the focus of the group can all go toward each member contributing what they can to enriching the group, rather than toward maintaining their position in the pecking order.

Further Principles

25.

Keep their attention on you

It doesn't really matter why their attention is on you, just make sure it is. This is especially true in the beginning, while you're still gaining the kids' trust and respect (see also tool 12, "Attach the kids to you," page 96).

I had a group that spoke in a lot of texting acronyms (ROFLOL, OMG, IMO, etc.) so I started translating all my sentences to acronyms: "IAGTDSFYWEBI!" They had no idea what I was saying, but it was a fun game joining in and adding to what they were already doing, and drawing their attention to me. Another time when our water break was over, and it was time to get hiking again, I started impersonating Bob Marley, but changing the lyrics: "Get up, stand up, stand up for the hike! Get up stand up, don't give up the hike!" This became a common theme song for me with many groups to come. Often students would ask, "Mark, how much farther do we have to hike?" If we'd been going for miles and were almost in camp I'd often say, "I'd guess we're about a tenth of the way there." I'd wear my clothes funny, make up strange dances, get everyone to yell at the top of their lungs, and generally do the unexpected in small ways that were fun for me.

These are just a few examples of how I kept their attention on me, keeping them guessing what I'd do next. It was also gratifying to model non-conformity in an age group where conformity is king (even though they often seem to be rebelling against it).

This principle of keeping their attention on you and doing the unexpected has many different possible expressions, depending on your personality style. You might stop the van and ask everyone to jump out, lie in the ditch, and jump back in the van again. It really doesn't matter. They'll call you crazy, and that's a good thing. Their attention will be on you and what unexpected thing you'll do next. If you're boring and you always give straight answers to questions, they'll soon tire of you, and turn their attention to what mischief they can think up to amuse themselves. A big part of being a good leader is being a good entertainer. Don't worry, the things you say and do can be horrible entertainment by any sane person's standards, but if they're out of the ordinary, playful, over the top, and confident, they will serve just great. Most important, if *you're* enjoying the process then you're golden. I was fine with the students laughing at me all they wanted. My job wasn't to make them my friends, it was to lead them. But in fact this kind of playfulness will tend to make the kids your friends. When the students are laughing at me, as long as I show them I'm fully comfortable with their laughter, I can only gain influence. They are looking to *me* for what happens next, and as a leader, that's exactly where I want them to be looking.

Once the kids are solidly with me, and accepting of my leadership, then I can guide more of their attention to themselves and each other, giving them more autonomy and choice as they become ready to express it in healthy ways. It's very important to keep their attention on you, but to be a successful teacher it's just as important to know when it's time to step aside and cultivate their own internal resources and independence. This avoids them putting you in the "God" role and following you—or whoever comes along next—blindly, no matter where they are led.

26.

Healthy venting

I found it very important to make sure the kids knew that all emotions were OK, and that feeling and expression are part of being human. While I would often let a kid vent at me (I could handle it), I would not allow kids to vent at each other, which wasn't ever useful. However I didn't want to give the impression that emotions are bad. Bottling up feelings is just as unhelpful as letting them explode in the face of another group member.

So I gave them other options for expression that didn't come at the expense of another group member. Breaking sticks, throwing rocks (away from the group) or yelling at the trees, were all healthy forms of venting that I encouraged with the kids.

Sometimes I sensed that an angry or frustrated kid wouldn't feel safe or comfortable being the only one to vent or yell at the top of their lungs, so I told the whole group we were all going to yell, and see how loud we could get! I knew we would all benefit, including myself. Once I did a role reversal and said, "*I* want to yell, we're doing this for me. But I won't feel comfortable unless we all do it. Everyone, line up on the ridge, that's right. On the count of three, let's see how loud we can get. Ready? One, two, three! Aaaaaaaaaaaaaaaaagghhh!" The kids did a half-assed job of yelling on the first round, so I said, "Come on, we can do louder than that. Again, ONE, TWO, THREE!! AAAAAAAAAAAG-GGGHHH!!!!" By the third or fourth attempt, most of us were screaming our heads off. When we finished, I was surprised how much better I felt! It was a nice reminder that we *all* can benefit from healthy expression.

27.

Don't forget those doing well

This is key. The kids that are doing well are your greatest allies. Give them as much of your attention and care as the kids demanding your attention through negative behaviors. If a problem kid is taking a higher percent of your energy on a certain day, apologize to the kids who are doing well. Acknowledge how much you appreciate what they give to you and the group, and that you'd much rather spend time having fun with them, or supporting them in their goals, than on solving problems. "Tonight Kevin is really hurting and needs extra attention. I'll be sure to give the rest of you more attention down the line because I know you all deserve equal support in achieving your own goals."

28.

Don't do tasks for the kids just because it would be easier for you than letting them struggle

I can't tell you how much time I spent standing by watching the kids utterly fail at simple group tasks that would have taken me minutes to complete. Yet as much as possible, I wouldn't step in..

Once I waited for a good hour and a half as my group tried to figure out how to tie a rock to a rope, then throw that rope over a tree branch so that we could all hang our food and go to sleep. I could have saved myself that hour and a half by simply doing it for them in a few minutes, but that would have robbed them of the whole point of wilderness therapy. The group got frustrated, attempted to give up, asked me to do it. I just replied in good humor, "This isn't a very difficult task. If you guys work together you can figure this out." They gave another feeble attempt and once again the rock slipped out of the poor knot they'd tied in the rope. They implored me to just do it for them. This time I said, "If you want to earn some independence going on overnights with your family this family week, let's see some independence. I'm not here to do every little thing for you guys." They tried again, failed again. They whined, "We're never going to go to bed! We're never going to finish this!" To which I said, "I'm comfortable with that."

Eventually they did get the food hung, and we all finally went to bed.

This may seem like a small thing, but it's not—not if it's done in a supportive way. By not helping the kids in a simple task that any group of (whole and healthy) human beings is capable of, I was showing faith in their own abilities and giving them space to succeed. That will translate into a lot of other areas. If they were dysfunctional enough as a group that they *didn't* succeed at a group task, this would also be a useful learning experience. I would likely make it the topic of our next Group, and soon they *would* succeed at their group tasks, learning how to work together.

29.

Exaggerate

Want a way to empathize with the kids without getting all serious and dour? Exaggerate.

I often had groups that would complain about how awful Monarch was. Some staff would be tempted to argue that Monarch is a great opportunity for them, but that would fall on deaf ears. If they aren't experiencing it as an opportunity, they certainly won't if you waste their time trying to convince them with words. So instead I would often empathize and have fun by exaggerating—complaining way better and bigger than they were. I had fun trying to think up problems that they had never even considered:

"I know," I'd say, "this place is horrible! Your parents thought you were at risk before you got sent here, now all you have between you and a hungry bear is a piece of fabric! But better a fast death than the slow death likely to set in due to hypothermia since this chintzy program's raincoats are probably going to dissolve under the first rain. It's amazing I'm still alive! I have to do this every three weeks, and if you think they pay me well out here, think again! Then there's giardia, if the rain doesn't get us it'll be the water we drink, slow death from shitting diarrhea all over the place!"

Exaggeration is also a great way to give a kid greater awareness without having to explain. When kids didn't let up on the whiny questions such as, "How long 'til we get there," "I'm tired," etc. I'd have fun mirroring it back to them, but exaggerated. "C'mon, c'mon, how long 'til we get there?! Are we there yet? What about now? Now are we there? How many more miles? I asked you two minutes ago but now I want to know again because I don't actually listen to anything you say—I just like asking you every three steps because it takes my mind off how incredibly exhausted I am!!!" Playing the role of the complaining kid helps me join them in a fun way and avoids the surface-level question of "how much longer?" that really has nothing to do with what's going on. If that was the real question, they would have asked only once, and listened to my answer. But perhaps more important, playing the role of the complaining kid helps them see, and *experience,* their own behavior from the outside, giving them a useful perspective.

As long as you do this kind of exaggeration with warmth in the heart and a twinkle in the eye, as my provocative therapy friend and colleague Nick Kemp would say, it really shifts people to a better place, without ever having to explain anything. Instead the lesson comes through *direct experience.* You can do this with any behavior that seems to be unhelpful for a person or a group.

One time Molly and I had a group of kids that got really overboard with swearing, so rather than demand an end to it, we both started cursing up a storm while we cooked our meal that night.

"These are some fucking shitty beans!" Molly yelled.

"Yeah, bitch fuck shit! This dinner is gonna taste like Deer twat!!" I replied.

"Yeah, this fucking bitch of a fire is gonna shit all over my fart!!"

"What the fuck is this shitty tarp leaking rain on us like horse piss all over my face!!!!"

"Ass fucker!! No shit, fucking shit fuck!!

"Deer twat fucking ass lick cock!!"

The kids thought this was the most hilarious thing they'd ever heard, and for Molly and I, it was surprisingly therapeutic. After this, Molly and I called a Group and we shared how our experience was that the group was in a more negative space than usual with all the swearing going on. Most of the group agreed, and we decided to stop the swearing for everyone's benefit (not because Molly or I arbitrarily decided that swearing was "bad"). It's another example of focusing on the natural consequences: people getting in a negative headspace due to the swearing.

30.

Swearing

My approach on swearing as a form of expression was to keep it to a minimum, but not worry about it being an absolute minimum, as long as it wasn't directed at an individual. The important thing was that we agreed as a group what kind of environment we wanted to create for ourselves. If swearing got out of hand, it tended to get the group in a more negative space, so I would bring this up as a concern and ask that they cut back on swearing. (Again, this is focusing on the natural consequences of swearing).

What I also explained was, "We have our own group culture in the wilderness, which is the result of how we choose and agree to interact with each other in the most supportive way for us. Out in society there are certain norms of respect that it's important to go along with even if they are different than our group norms. If we're OK with occasional swearing in our group, that is OK with me as long as you all agree to have no swearing in public where others might be offended by it, such as when we're stopping for gas on our way to our expedition site." If students couldn't control themselves in public, then I'd ask that they not swear at all until they learned to have control over it.

What I was absolutely intolerant of was any swearing directed at another student.

"Fuck you, Toni!" Seth said once when she gave him the stink eye for being a slow hiker as we trekked through a particular steep section of trail.

"Hold on," I said, halting everyone. "Seth, it sounds to me like you're really angry. We can have a Group and take all day to work this out if that's necessary, but I don't want anyone in this group to be swearing at anyone else. No matter how angry we may get with each other at times, it's important that we always be able to speak to each other with respect as we work out our differences."

Usually this would work great, and from here I'd support Seth and Toni in communicating clearly with each other about their needs and requests until we had a satisfactory arrangement between them. If Seth refused not to stop swearing, then I'd ask him to go on solo and stay removed from the group until he was ready to either stay quiet in the group or speak with respect to other group members.

31.

Don't forget to ignore

With all these tricks and tools of how to be creative, use humor, empathize, facilitate ritual, do the unexpected, try something else, it's important to realize that these are all different forms of engagement. Yet sometimes the best thing to do is to ignore behavior.

If behavior is clearly excessive attention-seeking or an attempt to get a reaction out of you, it can be very useful to ignore it. If you ignore a behavior, and the kid abandons the behavior, problem solved. Once there was a kid who kept asking me lots of useless questions in camp. At a certain point I just pretended I couldn't hear him anymore. If he happened to ask something legitimate, I would turn to him, look him in the eyes, and answer the question, but any of the useless stuff I just ignored. Pretty soon he stopped asking the useless questions because I demonstrated to him that they were, indeed, useless, which is very different from just talking about it.

Kids will try to get reactions out of you all the time, and a lot of the time it's just not worth responding to. Once a girl was frustrated with me when I asked her to dig the latrine as her chore.

"Where's the fucking shovel?" she asked me.

"Good question," I said in my most ordinary voice, "The shovel is right over there." I pointed and turned to assign the other chores. She grumbled and went to grab the shovel. She came back to me with the shovel and said, "Can I go fucking that way to dig the fucking latrine?" She pointed toward some pines with her middle finger.

"Yes, good idea," I responded after counting heads and making sure none of the other students was off peeing. She went off to dig the latrine and got much more benefit taking her anger out on the dirt than she would have gotten from me making a fuss about her swearing.

Waiting for "contact," as described earlier, (tool 10, "Wait for "contact,"" page 92) is a way of ignoring all the mental arguments and meanings and interpretations about the past or future that a kid may use to try to hook you. Any time we ignore one thing, we have room to pay attention to something else, in this case acknowledging the deeper communication from the them: that they're angry. Rather than getting hooked into attempting to have a rational conversation with words that are coming from an emotional place, we can be more respectful by ignoring the words and acknowledging their emotion in the moment: "I get that you're really experiencing a lot of anger right now."

When a kid is being a nuisance, especially if I don't know them, my preference is not to ignore but to go straight for the scary stuff (tool 9, "Go towards the scary stuff," page 90). Especially at the beginning, ignoring their behavior too often could be understood as them "winning" and me "not knowing what to do." Whereas if I do something to engage them, it shows I'm in tune, intelligent, paying attention, and not afraid of them. It is also the beginning of the relationship, which is where all my influence is (tool 8, "Relationship is influence," page 87). But ignoring definitely has its place once you already have a relationship established with a kid. It's important to ignore a needy kid some of the time and give equal attention to the kids doing well (tool 27, "Don't forget those doing well," page 142).

Once I had a particularly vocal kid constantly asking how much longer we had to hike: "How many more miles until camp?" James asked for what seemed like the hundredth time.

"Do you guys hear something?" I asked the rest of the group? Everyone quieted and listened.

"What was it like?" Someone asked.

"Like kind of a squawking bird or something," I said, "It sounded pretty close."

We started hiking again. Then James piped up with another question: "Is the rest of the hike going to be this steep? Or does it get steeper?"

"Do you guys hear that?" I asked immediately. "It almost sounded like a human."

Again they'd heard nothing.

"So is it going to get steeper?" James asked again.

"There it is!" I exclaimed.

"Hey, stop, I'm serious!" James said.

"Kind of sounds like a mockingbird."

"No, no, really…"

"Did you guys know that bird-song is either birds swearing at each other to leave each other's territory, or it's sweet-talking each other so they can get it on? Bow-chicka-bow-wow!! I wonder which one is going on here!"

James smiled and shook his head, "You're never going to tell me!"

"Sounds sexually excited to me," I said, continuing the game, "But I could be wrong, maybe it's wanting to fight." Other group members smiled or looked at me like I was a bit crazy. For the rest of the day, whenever James asked a question about the hike, I'd say again, "Do you guys hear something?"

If you ignore a behavior and the kid escalates the behavior in a way that can't be ignored, try paying attention to it in a way they aren't expecting. Consider holding a Group and giving the kid way more attention than they ever wanted. Ignoring really is just the act of re-focusing your attention. There are plenty of unhelpful habits kids have, whether unintentional or intentional, that will continue as long as you give them the kind of attention and response they're used to, or looking for. Not responding, or responding in an unexpected way changes the interaction.

32.

If it isn't working, try something else

Just because you start out with one strategy, doesn't mean you have to stick to it to the bitter end. If ignoring a kid isn't working, try humor or exaggeration. If that isn't working, try "contact" and communicate how what they're doing affects you. If that isn't working, hold a Group. The law of requisite variety states that, all else being equal, the element in the system with the most flexibility will have the most influence. Be the element with the most flexibility.

Josh was a little kid with curly brown hair. The night before, he'd completed his initial solo experience with another staff and been hiked in to join with our group. Now it was the next morning and he simply refused to hike. He wasn't angry, he'd just decided, "I don't want to be here, and I just don't see any point in hiking."

I didn't know much of anything about him yet, so I started out by learning about him, and why he thought his parents sent him. He was happy to tell me about things back home, concluding: "My parents just don't get me at all. They think I need to be here, and they're wrong."

"Well, I'm really sorry to hear your parents misunderstand you so completely. That sounds really tough. And I'm sorry you had to end up getting thrown in here with all of us on this hiking trip that seems so useless to you."

"I don't have anything against you or the other students," he said. "You seem like a nice guy. I just don't want to hike. My parents were wrong in sending me here. Feel free to go on without me."

"Well I won't do that, because like it or not, it's my job to keep everyone in my group safe, and that includes you. We'll all stay right here if we have to. But what about you? Sounds like your parents are clueless around what they want for you, but surely there must be things that you want. What's important to you, what are some of your goals?"

"My goals have nothing to do with being here," he said.

"What are some of your goals?"

"I want to finish high school and move out and go to college so I don't have to live with my parents anymore. It's just a matter of waiting until I'm old enough to be on my own."

"That sounds like a good goal to me. Given that your parents are so clueless about you and yet they also have the power to send you here against your will, do you think there's a chance we here at Monarch might be able to help them realize how clueless they are? Do you think there's a way that I or your therapists or both could help you finally have a voice with your parents so that they might finally actually hear your side of things? Then maybe you could leave this program sooner and get back to finishing high school and going to college and getting away from your parents."

"They're more clueless than that, they'll never get it," he said matter-of-factly. "I know you guys mean well, but they're just never going to get it."

"What gives you the impression they won't ever get it…?" I found out more detail about his experience and how he drew his conclusions, I empathized, and I probed for what he wanted and how I might be able to help him get that, but he remained unconvinced that I or Monarch could have anything to offer him. It always ended up with, "I don't mean to mess up your day and the rest of the group, my parents just should never have sent me here."

"I get that you don't see any use in hiking for your own goals. Would you be willing to do it for the rest of the group? A lot of the group members here have goals with their families that involve completing the hiking portion of this expedition so that they can have time with their families. Even though you don't want to hike and see no use in it yourself, would you be willing to hike so the rest of the group can accomplish their goals for this expedition?"

He shook his head.

"Would you be open to hearing from another kid in the group, to learn more about the group we have going here?" I said.

"Sure."

"I asked Andy—a kid who had initially had a lot of resistance to the program, but was now gaining a lot of benefit—to come and share with Josh about his own experience. After Andy and Josh had connected, Josh remained un-swayed.

By now the rest of the group was all packed up and ready to hike. I asked my co-instructor, Trina, to try her luck with Josh, hoping he would respond better to her. No such luck.

After Trina had talked with Josh almost as long as I had, I came back and tried humor, exaggerating how fun the hike would be, telling him that most likely when he was a great-grand-father he'd be telling his grand kids about the incredible adventure he went on with Mark and Trina and the Monarch March of Mountain Madness. He smiled, but still calmly shook his head. I asked him if he would do the hike for me, or if he saw any benefit in simply getting the exercise. "No," and "No." But he assured me, "It's nothing against you. You seem like a nice enough guy."

My co-instructor Trina tried everything she could think of too. At one point she picked up Josh's hiking boots and started using them like puppets. She wiggled one of the boots and in a high squeaky voice she said, "Hey Josh, let's go hiking!" Then she wiggled the other boot and said, "Yes! Will you put us on so we can go tromping around the mountains?" The other boot responded enthusiastically, "Yeah, that'd be just great! I sure hope you put us on today so we can go hiking!" "Yeah, yeah. Please put us on, Josh, we want to go hiking!"

Josh remained as amicable and unmoving as ever. Other than calling a Group with all the students, which at this point looked like it would also go nowhere, we had both pretty much run out of creative possibilities. I was beginning to think we'd be staying here for at least another night.

As Trina and I were both searching for our next move, Josh looked up at us and said, "OK, I'll hike."

"REALLY?" I asked, not bothering to hide the amazement in my voice.

"Yeah, I'll hike."

"Okay," I said. "I don't understand why, but I'm really appreciative that you're willing to hike."

"Ehh, why not?" he said.

"I'm appreciative too," Trina said. "You know I'd really hit the bottom of the barrel when I started performing a puppet show with your boots!"

Trina and I both started laughing at the hilarity of the scene we'd just been a part of. Josh smiled and started putting on his hiking boots, and he presented no further resistance for the rest of his time at Monarch.

Later when I asked Josh about what had changed his mind he said, "I just decided there was no point in staying there, so I figured I might as well just do the hike."

I can't claim that anything we tried in particular can be given credit for Josh deciding to hike, but it's a good example of creativity and flexibility in paying attention to a kid's needs, exploring possibilities, and committing fully to each, then abandoning it when it's clear it's not working. If Josh had still refused to hike, we would have stayed in camp and not pushed the hiking issue any more that day. Perhaps one of us would have taken a day hike with the rest of the group (allowing them to hike an equivalent amount to the originally planned expedition, so they could still earn time with their families) and the other stayed with Josh. This in itself would have been a good rapport move with Josh, showing him we weren't going to try to make him do the hike (something over which we ultimately had no control).

Self Care

33.

Dealing with your own "shit" that comes up

Your emotional buttons will be pushed and you will be triggered by kids. Teens are a fabulous pointer towards our own unfinished business and growth points. When you recognize this is how it is, you don't have to try to hide anything, just be aware of it, and have your own support/therapy outside the work setting. Don't turn to the kids for support in solving your personal problems; that's your job.

However, letting the kids know that you get your own therapy and support, similar to what they're doing is a fabulous model for them, showing them that we're all human, and that strong leaders can be even stronger by doing their own personal growth, and by being totally OK being vulnerable and open to new learning.

If you find yourself wanting the kids to like you, or not liking the kids who don't like you, then you have a problem. What's necessary is for you to like them; they don't need to like you back. If you find yourself wanting the kids to like you, get this handled on your own. You might ask yourself, "Do I experience a need for the kids' approval?" "Do I have a need to be helpful and solve their problems?" All these "needs" are points of leverage that the kids will be very good at noticing, and they'll use them to manipulate you. (See tool 45, "Manipulation," page 202.) Try changing these "needs" to "wants," and realize that most of the time you won't get them from the kids (tool 4, "There is no *need* or *have to,*" page 71). It's not the kids' job to acknowledge your awesomeness; be sure not to put that burden on them along with everything else they're already dealing with.

Any time the kids ask you about your own experience, you don't have to answer it. Ask yourself, "Would sharing this with them help them with their process?" If so, by all means share your experience. But if you find yourself wanting to share or talk about yourself to emote or work through your own problems, this is not the place to do it. All sharing of your own experience should be in support of the kids.

The kids would always ask me if I did drugs, and what kinds I did, etc. One response you can always use is, "Convince me how answering that question is relevant to your own process, and I'll answer it." When kids ask you these tough personal questions often it's to get leverage, "If you did drugs why are you telling me I can't do drugs?" My answer was always this, "I never said you can't do drugs. You're here because you have stuff to work out with your parents. They don't want you doing drugs. If you care about having a relationship with them, and all the benefits they provide for you, the drug issue is going to be an important thing to work through with them. As long as you're at Monarch we have a no-drug rule, and of course what you do on your own time once you leave Monarch is your own business."

When kids asked me about my drug use, I usually answered with honesty, "I've tried a few drugs, just marijuana and alcohol, to see what the experience was like. I didn't find the experiences all that great, and not worth the risk to my body of doing it more than a few times."

Another possible response is exaggeration: "Oh, yeah. I do everything, Crack-cocaine, PCP, E, marijuana, paint huffing, glue, oxycontin, prescription, non-prescription, meth, LSD, and scratch and sniff stickers. Did you bring any scratch and sniff stickers?" (Tool 29, "Exaggerate," page 145.)

34.

Caring for yourself so you can care for the group
(And caring for the group, so you can care for yourself)

The emergency instructions in airplanes tell you to put on your oxygen mask first, before assisting others. The principle is the same when working with teens. To the extent possible, do everything you can to make sure that you are warm, properly clothed, well fed, and well rested at all times. It's a very simple idea that lots of people in this profession overlook, because most people in this profession are drawn to this kind of work by a desire to help others. Don't fall into the trap of wanting to help the kids so much that you realize only after it starts raining that your own tent isn't set up and your rain jacket is at the bottom of your pack. Accidents and conflicts are much more likely to happen when people are low on sleep, food and shelter. If you haven't thought ahead to care for yourself, you won't be able to properly care for the group. They deserve your best.

At the same time, it's important to avoid doing anything for yourself in a way that is perceived as taking *away* from the group. Don't do anything for yourself that compromises the kids' needs. For example, I would take along some specialty food items for myself that the kids didn't have access to (particularly my coveted Sri Ra Cha chili sauce). When the kids complained about not having it for themselves, I framed it in their interests: "This is my job and I'm out here longer than any of you, and I assure you I'm a much better and happier leader for you all when I can carry along some of the food that I like. I'd be happy for you all to have hot sauce too, but they don't pay me enough to buy it for everyone. With a bit of persistence, you can finish this program, go home, and come back and get a job here as a field instructor and use your money to buy and carry around whatever food you want to eat!" (Tool 2, "Frame everything in their interests," page 62.) Their usual response was something like: "No way! The last thing I'd do in my life is be a field instructor!" So it turns out I was sacrificing quite a lot to be their leader, even if I did have the perk of being able to buy my own hot sauce.

While you want to make sure you always cover your most basic necessities (food, warmth, shelter, hot sauce), consider giving up most of your other non-basic "needs"—at least temporarily. This Buddhist approach is not only quite practical, but often much easier. For example, am I going to have a better day if I stop and get an ice-cream cone for myself and eat it in front of the kids? Maybe. But maybe I'll have an even better day if I stop and play Frisbee with them instead—and avoid riling them up about the ice cream.

35.

Getting good sleep

This is probably the most important aspect of taking care of yourself so you can take care of the kids. Without sleep, even the most competent people become increasingly inept. One of the most common things my fellow field instructors complained about was not being able to get good sleep due to worrying about the kids. Here was my strategy for getting good sleep almost every night I worked.

1) *To prevent worrying about their physical safety:* Before I went to bed, I would take extra care and spend extra time doing whatever I thought was best in order to set the stage for success. For example, I would make sure I was comfortable with the distance between the girls and boys camps. I would have possible trouble-makers camp near me. I would take the shoes and socks of possible run risks and maybe tie their tent zippers to mine. I made sure everything about camp was within policy, and I also made sure that everything was set up in the way that I felt would best support success.

In order to do my job and keep my sanity and health, I needed sleep. My job description did not include being a night watchman. If parents wanted their kids to have zero chances of screwing up, they could have sent them to lock-down facilities where they'd be utterly controlled and learn nothing. At Monarch, kids had the opportunity to screw up and learn from it, or not screw up and build trust. When kids snuck out at night there were natural and logical consequences of running away, or having sex, which were both inevitabilities for some kids, just as they are inevitabilities for many kids who don't go to programs like Monarch. (Read more on this topic in Chapter Two, "The Trip that Lives in Infamy.") Getting good sleep involves accepting these inevitabilities and *relaxing*. No matter what comes up, you'll be the best support to the kids when you have a full night's sleep. After I did a final round to make sure everyone was in their tent, I would curl up in my tent and go to sleep, at peace with the reality that if students decided to sneak out in the middle of the night, they could easily do so without my knowledge or ability to stop them.

2) *To prevent worrying about their psychological well-being:* Often field instructors would lose sleep not over whether a kid might run off or try to have sex, but rather whether they would be OK psychologically. Aside from taking suicide precautions, when appropriate, it's again important to let go of all aspects that you don't actually have any control over (which is a lot of it). Remember the saying, If you have a problem you can do something about, you don't have a problem. If you have a problem you can't do anything about, you don't have a problem. If you don't take credit for a kid's successes (perhaps because of a "need" to be good at your job?), then you don't need to take the blame for their failures either. You're there for support, period. If you provide that, you are successful in your work, even if a kid kills himself.

3) *To prevent losing sleep over constantly reviewing how I can improve as a leader:* If you are being kept awake by thinking about what all you're learning, and how you can do better the next time, you may want to set aside a specific time during each day that you will devote to reflection and your own learning process. (Of course it's also very important to have some time for yourself when you do something completely unrelated, such as reading a novel or staring at the clouds or whatever works for you to completely forget about the kids and their problems for a little while). After I have some time for reflection, if I still find something running through my mind at night, preventing me from going to sleep, I'll write it down on paper. Since it's written down, I know I won't forget it, and I can pick up thinking about it the next day. This allows me to let go of it for the moment, so I'm free to drift asleep. Often the next day I'll find that the answers to the problem come more easily after a full night's sleep.

More About Having Fun

36.

Humor

Find your own style. My particular style comes out in a lot of these examples that I share. There are lots of recipes for humor, but relatively few common ingredients, to many people's surprise (see the next tool for those ingredients). One common misconception about humor is that many people think being humorous requires telling jokes, like a stand-up comedian. This is only one kind of humor, and it isn't for most people. It certainly isn't my style. Unless this is already your style, don't worry about thinking up jokes, which are a one-way form of entertainment (I create and deliver a joke and you laugh). Instead, get curious about how you can discover the two-way humor that naturally arises in a relationship when you let it (we *both* laugh and discover and build a joke together based on the present moment).

One time we were in particularly remote area of wilderness, or so we thought. Suddenly, out of nowhere, we hear chainsaws shattering the pristine quiet of the backcountry. "Listen," I said, "it's the mating calls of the black bears." Another intense whining sound deepened into a throaty grind. "Oh boy, he sounds in the mood!" "Those aren't bears," one student said. "Wow, that bear must be looking for a hot mama bear!" another student joined in the joke and we all started laughing—the noise sounded so primal and sexual. "He's definitely on the prowl," I agreed as the whirring and grinding intensified further. "Oh yeah mama bear, come to big daddy bear!" "Do you think he's found a mate yet?" another student asked. Just then the chainsaw must have hit a really knotty section of wood, because the sound shifted to intense, deep, grinding pulses. "Oh boy, I think he just has!" I said, and we all lost it.

Much of this two-way humor will never be funny, ever again, to anyone else. This kind of humor arises out of the moment, we enjoy it, and then it's gone. Many of the best of these moments I couldn't even write down and have you understand—they are the "You had to be there," kind of moments.

If you want to bring more of this two-way playfulness, creativity, and humor into your everyday life, start by reading the next tool. Then get the improv book "Truth in Comedy." But to really get this you need to go beyond reading. To learn all kinds of incredible things about two-way playfulness (and have a great time), take an improv theater/comedy class or join an improv Meetup group. I've gained more social skills and achieved more personal development through doing improvisational theater/comedy than any other single thing. Plus, it's a lot of fun!

37.

Be creative:
(The ten commandments of
improvisation)

Being creative with someone else (two-way creativity) is all about improvisation. Below are the basic rules of good improvisational theater/comedy. I've found that the same elements that go into creating a great improv scene also go into creating a great life. After all, life is just a long story composed of scene after scene of improvisation. Here are the 10 commandments of improvisation* as I applied them to my interactions with kids:

---

* These commandments are adapted from a Xeroxed list I received in my college improv group. It didn't include a source, so I'm not sure in which book these commandments were originally printed. Various versions of the ten commandments of improvisation are available on the internet.

1) *Thou shalt not deny (Though shalt "Yes, and")*: This is the most important rule of improvisation. In a childcare context, there are plenty of areas where you are going to be saying "no" for purposes of safety and the interests of the group. So don't say "no" anywhere else that you don't have to. Instead, if a student offers something, say, "Yes, *and*" then add to it:

Mark, can we build a dam?" "Yes, sounds like fun…, and let's see if we can make a pool large enough to take a good bath in."

"I heard a joke, you want to hear it?" "Yes…, and after that I have one for you."

"That tree over there looks like a dolphin!" Now you might look at that tree and see nothing like a dolphin in it. However if you say, "That doesn't look like a dolphin to me; I see a bearded man," this kind of comment—being honest where you don't need to be—has the effect of shutting down the other person, and shutting down the playful, creative process of the group. Instead why not say, "Yeah, I can see that!" (If you give it a go you can see almost anything). Then add, "And that rock over there looks like a toad!"

2) *Thou shalt listen actively*: The application of this improv rule with kids is pretty obvious. They want to be heard. A lot of people think creativity is about talking more and thinking up clever things to say, but creative people learn to listen carefully, to empathize, and to trust. Only from there can you "Yes, *and*—."

"Mark, I can't believe you're making me count out loud when I go off to pee. That's total harassment of my privacy! It's not like I'm gonna run away, we're in the middle of the wilderness!"

"I hear you, Lori. It sounds like you'd *really* rather not count out loud when you go off in the trees to pee. *Especially*, when we're all the way out here where you wouldn't possibly run away. It seems like a pretty basic thing for me to just let you go off to pee without having to shout out numbers every ten seconds."

"Yeah, exactly!"

"It's probably also pretty frustrating having to count out loud here just because you ran away a few times at home, even though that was a different situation and your parents are different people from me."

"Yeah, why should I be punished for running away from home, you would have run away from there too!"

"I bet you're right. And I agree, I don't want you to feel like you're being punished at all. That's not the point of this at all. The purpose of the counting is so I know where you are, so I can keep us all together and safe as a group. Once we get to know each other better, maybe it won't be necessary anymore. Until then, can you think of a way you can let me know where you are that doesn't feel like a harassment of your privacy?"

"Yeah, I tell you where I'm going, and promise I'll be back in five minutes."

"Maybe for the future, for now I want some way that I can hear where you are every ten seconds or so, so I'm not breaking Monarch policy. You can sing if you want."

A glint came into her eye. "OK!" She turned around and walked into the trees singing:

"You keep saying, you got something for me
Something you call love, but confess...
You've been messin' where you shouldn't have been messin'
And now someone else is getting all your best...

As she disappeared into the pine and juniper, she belted out:

"These boots are made for walking
And that's just what they'll do...
One of these days these boots
Are gonna walk all over you!

Yeah, you keep lyin' when you oughta be truthin'
And you keep losing when you oughta not bet...
You keep samin' when you oughta be a changin'
Now, what's right is right but you ain't been right yet!

*These boots are made for walking
And that's just what they'll do…
One of these days these boots
Are gonna walk all over you!!"*

The next time I went to pee, I sang a song too ("yes *and*ing" her earlier singing). This became a new game in the group, and pretty soon other kids were enjoying coming up with songs to sing as they went off to do their business!

3) *Thou shalt make the other look good*: By always making the other look good, defensiveness falls away and the whole person can come forward to contribute and be a creative part of the group. Once I had a group all throwing rocks as far as we could across a river. One kid was weak and when he threw a rock it splashed in the river, not even making it across.

"Tim can't even make it across the river!" One of the kids taunted.

Ignoring this, I reversed what had been described as a failure by "yes *and*ing," Tim's "mistake," thus recategorizing it as a success: "Good idea, Tim!" I said. "Let's see how big of a splash we can make with the smallest rock possible!" (We all had small rocks in our hands because we had been going for distance). I threw my small rock into the river as hard as I could, making a tiny splash. Soon the kids were all throwing tiny rocks into the river, making splashes, then one kid started skipping rocks, another started throwing in big rocks. We all had a great time together—including Tim instead of excluding him.

Another time we were hiking in a snowy area, and a kid's foot punched through the packed layer and he went into the snow up to his knee. Someone laughed at him. I said, "Who can post-hole the deepest?" It became a game of who could punch the farthest down through the snow crust—reversing the meaning of the post-hole from a mistake to a success.

I also gave kids recognition for their accomplishments and contributions whenever I noticed them. "Great job on the hike today, you were a great leader!" "Valerie, thanks for being there for Jill, I think she really appreciated your support today." "What a fabulous dinner, you're a really good cook!" Etc.

4) *Thou shalt seek to discover rather than try to invent*: This is a freeing attitude that takes the pressure off. The humor is already present to be discovered, you don't need to make it up, it's just about noticing the humor as it arises and joining in. Once we were hiking along and a student tripped on a rock, crossed his legs, and fell down on one forearm. He looked like he was in a break-dance position. "Nice break dance move!" I said, after I saw from his face that he was OK. After that he became known as break-dance-Nick, a title that he bore with pride!

Another time I meant to say, "Time to get the food ready to cook," but instead I said, "Time to get the cook ready to food."

"Time to get the cook ready to food!" I repeated my mix-up, and the kids laughed. "Who's the cook tonight?" I asked.

"Hank is," someone said.

"Hank," I said, "It's time to get you ready for food. I've decided to switch things up and have you eat all the food tonight. The rest of you, don't worry, you'll get your chance to eat everyone's dinner when you're cook. It will give you each a much stronger incentive to cook a good meal if you have to eat it all."

"Nice," Jacob said, "I call Mac and Cheese for my night, so I can eat it all!"

"Plus," I said, "there are seven of you, so that's perfect. You'll each get one huge dinner per week."

Andy said, "Yeah, like boa constrictors, they can survive months on one meal."

"There you go," I said, "you'll be doing much better than boa constrictors."

Discovering this kind of humor happened many times a day out in the field, in small ways, many of which would not be funny if I tried to explain them here, but they were enjoyable and often very funny in the shared moment. Having an attitude of discovering rather than inventing keeps you in the moment watching and listening to what's happening, keeping the space open to co-create with those present (rather than being stuck in your head inventing something in your own world). For more on this, reread the previous tool 36, "Humor," page 170.

5) *Thou shalt be specific and obvious*: Creativity is about specificity, and specificity is funny. If a student is acting out and I want to join them in that role and exaggerate it, notice the difference between these two:

"Oh, yeah, I know. This place totally sucks! It's really bad here. I don't like Monarch at all. This is a horrible fucking place!"

That's OK, but not nearly as effective in capturing the imagination as when you add in a few details:

"Oh, yeah, I know. This place sucks a marmots balls! It's so bad here it makes federal prison look like a vacation. I've met the devil and this place is worse than his bathroom!" (See tool 29, "Exaggerate," page 145.)

Don't get too worried about exactly what to say. The spirit of the emotion that comes through, and your full commitment, is much more important than the words.

6) *Thou shalt find something physical to do*: We are physical creatures, and there's a reason we enjoy seeing physicality in improv scenes. We enjoy even more *being* physical, and that's one of the advantages of a wilderness program. Being physical is a natural part of every day (hiking, digging the latrine, hanging the food). In addition to this it can be great to bring a hacky-sack or football along. You can also make up your own games and challenges like trying to catch minnows in the stream, or building a snow shelter that can fit a whole person inside. There are also lots of games you can play (searchable on google or created on the spot) that involve the whole body moving. "Bear, Ninja, Cowboy" is a kind of full-body Rock, Paper, Scissors. "Yeehaw" is a fun game of passing the focus around the circle using western themed body postures such as "Stern as a mule!" "There's a snake in my boots!" and of course, "Yeehawwww!!" There are

many more. These physical games can be a lot more fun than just sitting around in camp talking, especially if it's cold.

7) *Thou shalt seek out and get into trouble*: Our natural instinct is to avoid trouble. The creative person does the opposite and seeks it out. The earlier you confront life's series of problems the more in control and creative you will be. When I came on shift one time, a new girl whom I hadn't met before was now a part of the group. Lora glared at me and everything around her. She positioned herself a bit away from the rest of the group, brooding with her shoulders hunched. I walked right up to her and said, "Hey, I'm Mark."

"Fuck off," she said.

"I'm sorry you're here," I said. "Obviously you don't want to be here, and you don't want me to be here either I'm guessing."

"You're a smart one," she said sarcastically.

"I can put a thing or two together," I said. "I want to let you know that I can give you space, if that's what you ask for. I'll do everything in my power to make this place less of a hell for you. One thing I won't do, though, is fuck off, because believe it or not, I'm not doing this job for the great pay—."

"Yeah," she interrupted me, "You're doing it so you can feel good about yourself bossing around kids like me."

"Well there is that, too," I said. "I'm also doing it because I care about you guys, and I want to support everyone in my group. You don't need to take my word for it, you can find out for yourself if you think it's true, or if all I do is mess with you guys. I like to have a good balance of the two."

"Yeah, like ninety-five percent bossing kids around and five percent supporting."

"Five percent is kind of a lot, don't you think? Last expedition I was doing more like three, but I guess it could be five. Would you give me a gold star if I do five?"

She smiled for a moment before returning to her scowl, so I knew I was making a connection.

Here I'm also playing the role she cast me in, "yes *and*ing" her reality and showing my strength through no need to defend.

(See tool 46, "Roles," page 208.) It always seems easier (at first) to give in to our natural instinct to avoid trouble, but simply ignoring the glaring kid and hoping she will get over it, will only create bigger trouble later. Seeking out and "getting into trouble," allowed me to be creative in connecting with her, the only way through which I'll ever have any influence with her. (See tool 9, "Go towards the scary stuff," page 90.)

8) *Thou shalt rejoice in mistakes*: This is a liberating concept. You don't have to worry about getting into trouble when you expect and *want* to make mistakes. After all, if you're not making mistakes, you're probably not making anything worthwhile. When you accept mistakes as a desired part of the learning process, you become a role model to the kids showing that it's OK for them to make mistakes (and thus they are freed to actually *do* and *create,* just as you are).

Just as you make the students look good by turning their mistakes into successes, you can do the same with your own "mistakes." Once I was a little frustrated with the group not listening to me and I said, "C'mon, it's time to *gike!*" Somehow my brain combined the words "go", and "hike", and "gike" was what came out. I could have gotten defensive about this, and further frustrated, and worried that they might use it to make fun of me. Instead I said, "that's right, you all heard me, let's *gike!* We're gonna gike like we've never giked before. Let's show group B we're the strongest, best gikers this program has ever seen!" After that it became a running joke, and a new part of our regular vocabulary. I call this the jazz theory of life. If a jazz musician makes a mistake, as long as they make the mistake two more times, in a pattern, no one realizes it as a mistake. It becomes a new creative part of the musical composition.

One time one of my students let out a fart. He was a bit of a clumsy kid, already prone to becoming the butt end of the joke, so to speak. "Nice one!" I said, "The rice and beans speak again! Whoever can fart the loudest by the end of the day gets a chocolate covered almond! On second thought, there will be one prize for loudest, and another prize for smelliest!"

"Well *you're* going to win smelliest," one of the kids told me.

"Exactly!"

The rest of the day, no matter what was going on, the kids would drop everything to listen and judge the pitch, tone, and timbre of any new contender letting one rip. Soon we developed new winning categories such as "most musical," "creepiest," "nastiest," and "best improved."

The very best improv scenes I've seen, or been a part of, are the ones where a player makes a "mistake" and everyone treats that mistake as genius, building something incredibly creative and new from it. There are countless opportunities to do the same thing in life. When you or a student makes a "mistake," instead of letting this stay framed as a mistake, or even as a positive learning experience, try out receiving it as pure genius, "Yes, *and*" the mistake, and build a game out of it.

9) *Thou shalt commit thyself fully and courageously*: Give yourself fully to the process and relinquish control. (For more on relinquishing control, see tool 4, "There is no *need* or *have to*," page 71, and tool 3, "Power control battles," page 64.) Committing yourself fully and courageously to the present moment is something you can do consciously; let the rest happen. If you find this hard, remember the bit about rejoicing in mistakes. (For examples of full and courageous commitment see tool 23, "Take charge," page 129, tool 29, "Exaggerate," page 145, and pretty much everything else in this book.)

10) *Thou shalt trust thyself*: This comes full circle. Just as it is most important not to deny others, it is equally important not to deny *yourself*. Be sure that you "Yes, *and*" yourself just as you "Yes, *and*" others. Again, remember the bit about rejoicing in mistakes.

38.

Positive lying; telling tall tales

Positive lying is one improvisational game I liked to play with students.

One expedition we were sitting around the campfire in a grove of aspen and pine. Two new kids had just been hiked in to join our group after having finished their solo experience with another staff member. I introduced them to my group, and they started helping us collect and break firewood for the coming night.

A conversation started about how long various kids had been in the program, and the new kid, Brian, asked me what kid had been here the longest.

"Well, do you mean just as a student, or as staff also?"

"What do you mean?" he asked me.

"Well I was here as a student for a long time," I said. "That was many years before I became staff."

"You were a student here?" Henry, the other new student asked me. "Why were you here so long?"

39.

Earning vs. taking away

Y ou are He (or She) who giveth, *not* He (or She) who taketh
away. (See tool 12, "Attach the kids to you," page 96.) Your
job is to always give to the kids, never to take away. How is this
possible, you might ask? Easy, it's all a matter of how you describe it.

When I first started, it was assumed that if kids were good,
at the end of the expedition they would each spend four overnights with their parents. Kids were told, "As long as you do well
out there in the field, you'll get your four overnights with your
parents when we're back." When kids messed up or disregarded
too many rules, field staff would "take away" overnights (the
hidden presupposition being that every kid, upon entering the
program, had a right to four overnights as a default). Taking
away something that the kids already felt was theirs caused no
end of trouble and bad feeling.

To remedy this, all we did was change our *framing* of the
issue. We didn't get any easier on the kids; we just described it
differently. At the beginning of each expedition, kids were told,

"You have the chance to *earn* up to four overnights with your parents by the end of the expedition. If you are a team player, support the group, respect the field rules, and do your work, you will earn these overnights. Your field instructors will be noticing how much you do to earn these nights with your parents over the course of your expedition."

In the old framing the kids started out by looking forward to the four overnights they already felt *entitled* to. Then when they screwed up, they got mad when staff took their overnights away.

With the new framing, kids commonly asked me throughout the expedition, "Mark, do you think I've earned my overnights?" To which I responded, "If you continue helping out the way you have been, you will."

Framing overnights as something to be earned kept the kids focused on a positive goal that truly was motivating to them—a new orientation that will serve them well in many other situations.

40.

It's not about the hike

Now I'm good in a debate, and flaws in logic are difficult to get past me. So when I began my work as a field instructor, I found it easy to point out to kids when their resistance didn't make sense, or when their arguments or objections actually supported what I wanted from them. Sometimes this worked, but a lot of the time it didn't. I'd spend an hour or more talking in circles and by the end we were just where we'd started. They just wouldn't see what made sense!

"I can't hike," "I'm too tired," "You're a bad leader," "Monarch hates kids," "This group hates me," "I can't cook." It turns out that these verbal complaints often have little or nothing to do with what's really going on. I remember the moment I learned this lesson.

It was the end of a long hike, and as we neared camp at the end of the day one of the students sat down and refused to go any farther. When I went back to see what was the matter she said, "It's too much. I'm too weak. I can't hike anymore."

This was not a weak girl, and this was not the first time she'd stopped. All throughout the day she'd been refusing to go on. Every time the whole group had been forced to stop with her, sometimes for hours. Each time we talked and talked about how we had to stay together as a group; we could go any pace as long as we kept going; after her strong hiking the day before it was clear that she was strong enough to make the hike; blah blah blah…

I was about to go down the same road again by pointing out to her that she was quite capable of going on. Then I stopped. She was sitting slumped over in front of me, head bent, brooding eyes downcast. When I took this in without her words, it was suddenly obvious to me that her objections had nothing to do with hiking or not hiking. In my arguing and reasoning with her throughout the day, I had completely ignored what she was really communicating. If anything my "reason" had only served to harden her in a stance that she never meant to take in the first place.

"Can you look at me?" I asked. This time when our eyes met I said, "You know, I've seen that you're very strong. We hiked some steep stuff today, and you were a trooper. I believe you could hike twice as far as today with a full pack on if you wanted to. So it's clear to me that this isn't about hiking; it's about something else, isn't it?"

She kicked a pinecone.

"I think something else is going on," I said, "Is it about home?"

She nodded, "I miss my mom."

We talked about that for a little bit, and I just listened to her. Pretty soon she got up and had no problem hiking the rest of the day.

If I had continued in my strategy of only responding to her words, we wouldn't have gotten into camp before dark, but more important, I never would have recognized what her real needs were. It seems obvious, but in this information age of print, e-mail, instant messaging, and text messaging, it can be easy to pay attention to the words alone and ignore all the non-verbal signals.

Since then I've usually been able to see past the words coming out of a kid's mouth, recognizing when their actions and expressions signal something much more important going on. Often I still didn't know what this was, but now I could ask. When I recognized and responded to this nonverbal communication, I'm sure it saved hours of useless discussion, but above all it was so much more respectful of the person. What better way to say, "I'm paying attention to you," than to recognize the conversation that, until now, no one realized was taking place?

One of the advantages of wilderness therapy is that the physical challenges often become metaphors for internal and emotional challenges. The physical challenges of the hike often bring out the internal turmoil, but if we fail to honor and empathize with the inner world, opportunities for growth are lost in the technicalities of "just finishing the hike." Empathy allows the student to feel the support they need to finish the hike, and successfully meeting the challenge of the hike becomes a metaphor for successfully navigating the challenges of their inner world.

41.

Nonverbal agreement

As mentioned in the previous tool, it is very important to pay attention to nonverbal communication. Only a small fraction of any communication is in the words alone. Much more is in the voice tone, the body stance, the eyes, etc. If a kid says she's fine and then rolls her eyes, you know she's not. If a kid has his arms crossed as he says he'll do whatever you ask, he probably won't. If the words say one thing, but the voice tone says another, the voice tone is where the truth is. If a kid says "yeah, totally," and he's looking at the woodpecker hammering away at the pine nearby, you might want to take a nature appreciation break before repeating yourself.

When I noticed a difference between the verbal and nonverbal communication of a kid, sometimes I would just verbalize what I saw: "Carey, I notice your arms are crossed, which makes me think you probably still don't agree with something. Is there something else important you want to say before you can feel good about the decision?" Other times I might not say anything overtly, instead stepping into their shoes and guessing at what might be bothering them, then checking that out with them. "Sarah, I think if I were you I'd feel like this decision is unfair, since you've contributed more than everyone else. Is that true for you?"

Sarah relaxed her crossed arms and said, "Well, I know everyone's helping out, so I guess I'm OK with the decision going forward." If her arms didn't relax, that would tell me there was still something to resolve. In this case, just acknowledging her extra contribution was enough.

42.

Projection

Projection is the phenomenon of understanding the world through our own experience. If a kid has an abusive uncle, and you happen to look like that uncle, your job is going to be harder than it otherwise would be. No matter how rational that kid is, he or she is going to respond emotionally to the similarity between you and the uncle. Remember this when kids act out the first few days that they're with you—whatever they say or do, it's probably not about you, it's about them. Show them that you aren't who they think you are.

Just as kids project on us, we also project on them. If you're particularly triggered by a kid, ask yourself, "What does this kid do that reminds me of something in my own life, past or present?" If a new kid reminds you of another kid with whom you had a particularly hard time, or of some other troubling person from your past, you will be likely to react out of your own past experience, rather than based on what's happening now with the unique person who is standing in front of you. If you realize you have a situation like this, it can be useful to check with your partner/colleague/co-instructor and see if they have the same reactions/intuitions as you do. You can also turn over any potentially difficult conversations with the kid to your co-instructor: "Hey Molly, I noticed I tend to get triggered when setting boundaries with Erin and I have trouble communicating cleanly with her. Would you be willing to talk with Erin about the importance of her staying in eyesight and earshot, and of asking permission before she disappears to go to the bathroom?" If the kid approaches you first, you can always find a valid reason to postpone a conversation a bit so you can collect yourself or enlist the support of your co-instructor: "Erin, I hear that this is really important to you. Right at the moment I'm low on blood sugar." (Or tired, or I have a headache, or I'm in the middle of setting up my tent, whatever's true.) "Do you want to see if another leader is available to talk with you now, or would you prefer to meet with me in a half hour after I've eaten? I think I'll be able to listen to you much better after I've gotten a snack." (Or rested, or taken some aspirin, or finished setting up my tent, etc.)

Even when we rationally recognize that someone reminds us of someone else from our past, that often doesn't change our emotional response to the similarity. And if a kid reminds you of a kid you really trusted and appreciated, be just as careful not to trust the new kid too quickly.

Projection can lead us to profound levels of empathy when our past experience applies to the present one, but it can also lead to confusion and misunderstanding when our past experience doesn't apply. Make your guesses about the kids you're working with, but don't forget to ask them if you're right, and don't get lax on rules and expectations just because you have a good feeling about a kid; build a relationship first.

43.

Tell a story

When you have a tidbit of wisdom to share, or a life lesson you want to pass on, or feedback for a student that you think they might be defensive about receiving, stop for a moment and see if you have a story or experience you can tell that conveys the teaching. Perhaps it's a story that happened to you, the moment when you learned something new. Perhaps it's a story of someone else that you heard, that really impacted you and taught you something.

If you tell a story of something that actually happened, it will be much easier for the listener to remember, and much easier for them to step into the story and get the learning themselves, as if the event happened to them. Everyone knows we learn best through direct experience, and a well-told story allows the listener to step into and experience someone else's learning as if it were happening to them. People *get* stories, in a holistic, embodied way that is much greater than the sum of its parts. It's no wonder that *story* is how people around the world have passed on their most sacred information from generation to generation for thousands of years. Our minds are built for story.

If a kid isn't cooperating, I could simply tell him or her, "Cooperating with the group will benefit you on the whole." And if I hear a kid blaming others I could say, "Instead of blaming, it works better if you tell the other person how you feel, and then make a request." If a kid is depressed and hating being in the program I could say, "I know it's hard now, but it will get better." These are the distilled concepts, easy to communicate, but not very convincing to the listener because they are stripped of all experiential basis.

The other option is I can tell a story, "George started out totally depressed too. He thought he could never fit in here. When he first joined the group he was miserable. Then he started to hear about the other kids in the group, and made some connections. He started making friends, and even though this still wasn't where he wanted to be, he found good things in being here. I bet he'd be willing to tell you about it, if you want. It's like that for a lot of kids who come here."

When a kid was struggling, I would frequently ask another kid doing well to share their own experience of how they got through the same thing. It was important to recognize that sometimes the kids were better resources for each other than I could ever be. After all, I've never been sent against my will to a wilderness program. What is my word worth when I tell an incoming student, "I know it's hard, but it will get better?" How could I know when I've never been through it? That's why it works much better to tell stories of the kids I've seen go through it, or better, have those kids tell their stories directly.

I can also tell a story about something I did go through, that was similar. In most ways I had a very supportive and fortunate life growing up, but this doesn't mean I can't relate to what these kids are going through. We're all human, and we all experience disappointment, loss, grief, betrayal, etc., even if we come from very different backgrounds. So I can tell a story about myself, "You know, I think we all have times in our lives when we feel really depressed, like nothing's going right and there's nothing we can do to make it better. When I first went to college I was worried I'd never fit in, never find a group of friends that I could really relate to. My whole first semester I never really found a group of people that I felt was where I belonged. It wasn't until four months later, in my second semester, that I finally found a group that I really connected with."

Another benefit of a story, besides being more believable and more understandable, is that a story allows someone the freedom to take or leave any possible teachings in the story. This makes it much more likely that they will take something. If you try to teach someone something about themselves directly, often they will be defensive and resist getting anything out of it.

Imagine you're a student who's unhappy and your leader tells you, "Cooperating with the group will benefit you on the whole." Or, "Instead of blaming it works better if you tell the other person how you feel, and then make a request." Or, "I know it's hard now, but it will get better." What is your initial reaction to that? For me the first two sound like lectures, which I don't like. The third one is a bit better, it starts by empathizing with my situation, but then I just have to take it on faith that things will get better? I'm resistant to that. Things aren't good now, so why would they get better?

Now imagine your leader tells a story of how they were also unhappy once, being in a group they didn't want to be a part of, yet eventually finding friends they never expected. Or your leader tells you they used to blame a lot, and then realized that their own feelings were up to them, even if someone did something they didn't like—that it was a lot easier to make requests and either have the requests granted, or if not to go meet their needs somewhere else. Or your leader tells you about how they were in a bad situation that they thought would never improve, and then they discovered a way that it could. How do you respond to hearing your leader tell these stories? For me I immediately relax. Now there's no pressure for me to change. I'm just hearing my leader tell me a story—complete with all the particular details—about how he or she changed, and how that was useful to them. I can take or leave whatever I want from the story, applying any learnings to my own situation based on what I think will be best for me. I can step into the shoes of my leader, experiencing what it was like for them to realize their mistake, or make a change. Just by doing that I'm beginning to gain that choice for myself.

More and more I notice that when I listen to someone else sharing their heart-ache, it will trigger certain memories and experiences from my life. I used to try to strip these stories down to the essence and just share the learning, but this robs the listener of the chance to have the learning for themselves. Now I make an effort to tell the story, even if it takes a bit longer, because it conveys so much more. That's why I've done my best to put plenty of stories and examples in this book.

More About Power Dynamics

44.

Triangulation

A lot of social interactions happen indirectly through another person: "Mark, Molly let me go to the bathroom without counting, why are you making me count?" Even though Molly isn't present, she is part of the interaction. (Every parent knows this one: "Daddy lets me do it.") "Mostly Molly and I are in complete agreement on supervision," I replied, "and sometimes we have slight differences in the details of what we're comfortable with. If Molly were here, she might not ask you to count, but this time you're stuck with me and I'm asking you to count." This takes Molly out the triangle, and makes it a direct interaction between me and the student.

Of course this also illustrates the huge importance of being on the same page with your co-instructor/partner as much as possible. The more this is the case, the less students will be able to triangulate to get what they want.

Triangulation also frequently happens between students: "Mark," William complained, "Dianna keeps flicking pinecones at me, make her stop!" My job here is to stay out of the middle of it, and instead support William and Dianna in communicating directly with each other until a resolution is reached. If I just told Dianna to stop throwing pinecones, this might work, but I'd be accepting the triangulation, robbing William of a chance to learn how to directly communicate what he needs with someone else. "Five-minute water break," I said. "Dianna, William has something to request of you." That took me out of the triangle, and supported each of them in expressing themselves while looking at each other, rather than looking at (and trying to act through) me.

Sometimes students would make some negative comment to a buddy about a third student. I wouldn't let this go unaddressed. Once as we were hiking I overheard Sam say to his buddy Henry, "Colin is such a pussy, whining about this hike. We haven't even gone a mile!" "Hey Sam," I said, "If you have something to say about Colin, I'd like you to communicate that directly to Colin. Do you have something you'd like to say to him?" "I just wish he wouldn't waste all our time going so slow," Sam told me. "I hear you. Let's take a five-minute break so you can tell Colin how you feel." Now that Sam was being heard by me (and his positive outcome of finishing the hike acknowledged by me), when he spoke to Colin about how he felt, his words came out much differently: "Hey Colin, I know it can be tough for kids when they first come in to the program. It was tough for me too. I just think you're plenty strong to do this hike, and it's better for all of us to just get the hike over with. It's less tiring to just get it done, and then we can have more time in camp." "Thanks, Sam," I said, "So after sharing your experience, do you have any request of Collin?" "Yeah, Collin, I'd really like it if you kept hiking like the rest of us when we're not on break, instead of always stopping to fiddle with your pack and stuff that slows us down."

45.

Manipulation

You need nothing from the kids, neither physically nor emotionally. This isn't being cold or hard-hearted, it's the opposite. It's freeing them from your own subtle manipulation of them. When you need nothing, you can have a genuine relationship based on building a positive interaction (you have fun + they have fun = everyone enjoys the connection, *or* you gain + they gain = everyone gains). When you trick yourself into believing you have needs that the kids should/have to satisfy, then you and the kids are in potential trouble. Rather than building a relationship around mutual gain, the relationship becomes built around canceling out a lack that you experience (I'll provide for the kids, as long as they meet my need to be liked = manipulation).

Feeling a need to be liked or appreciated by the kids was a common theme for new staff at Monarch. Your job with the kids is not to be liked, it is to unconditionally provide for their safety and wellbeing, (tool 12, "Attach the kids to you," page 96) and to be a role model. If you succeed in this, they may not like you, but they will love you—even if they may never realize it themselves, or show you in a way you can recognize. They may cuss you out the full length of your time with them. But you will remain a resourceful model for them for the rest of their lives. You are someone who showed up without trying to manipulate or control, something they may not have experienced from anyone before—someone who gave them the space and freedom to have their own experience and take charge of it.

So when you find yourself *needing* something from the kids, notice how you can instead meet your needs in a different relationship where it will be appropriate, or do your own personal work to let go of, or transform, your experience of the need. (See tool 33, "Dealing with your own 'shit' that comes up," page 160, and also tool 4, "There is no *need* or *have to*," page 71.) If you experience *needing* something from the kids, they have power over you. It's fine to *want* things from the kids; whether you get it or not, you're still OK. If you *need* something from them (for them to like you, appreciate you, help you), that poses a potentially major problem. The kids likely won't be willing to meet that need, or they may recognize it and use it to manipulate *you* (which they are very good at).

Once you have a good handle on not needing from the kids, what do you do when the kids still try to manipulate you? Mostly I didn't spend any time exposing or labeling kids' attempts to manipulate me. That would usually get into an argument about whether it was manipulation or not, which is often difficult to prove. And if you're wrong, you'll lose trust with the kids. It was much easier and more effective to simply find solutions to their "problems" that I suspected were really attempts at manipulating me. This worked great, because it turns out that fake problems have very easy solutions, *and* I never needed to worry about determining whether a problem was real or an attempt to manipulate. So when you suspect that a kid is trying to manipulate you, don't worry about exposing or confronting the manipulation, simply problem solve:

"My back is injured so I can't dig the latrine because it hurts my shoulder," Mary complained to me one day.

Now maybe this is true and maybe it isn't, but it doesn't matter. It's much easier just to problem solve than to question the legitimacy of what a kid is telling you, and set yourself up for a confrontation that may not have a clear conclusion. For example:

"I'm sorry to hear that, Mary, how did it happen?"

"It's an old injury"

"Can I take a look?"

"Sure, but you won't see anything."

"Was there something that made it act up again?"

"All the hiking."

"Well, I know you had a physical before coming into the field, and though it may hurt, the amount of weight we're carrying won't cause any further damage. The best way to reduce any inflammation is to put some snow in a zip-lock and ice it 20 minutes on, then 20 minutes off. As far as digging the latrine, do you want to see if someone else is willing to trade with you?"

"Whatever! You obviously don't care about us out here. I'll dig the latrine but if I injure myself it's your fault."

If this is a real issue for her, she'll be motivated to do the icing and find someone to trade chores with (or suffer the natural consequences of not doing so). If it's not a real issue for her, I've called her bluff in a way that she can't argue with. I've supplied reasonable solutions to her stated problem. More important, the reasonable solutions still allow her to hike, carry her weight, do her group chores *and* they make her life more difficult—having to ice 20 minutes at a time, something she probably won't want to do if it doesn't provide any benefit.

The next day Mary said, "Mark, my shoulder's even worse, I told you I shouldn't have dug that latrine."

"I was happy to arrange a change of chores, and you chose to dig the latrine," I said in response. "I also noticed you didn't ice it last night, which is the number one thing to do to help something like an inflamed shoulder. Do you want me to help you get an ice pack tonight?"

The tests will often keep coming, and you have to keep passing them, but there is no need to accuse a kid of lying or manipulating. Remember that even manipulation is a roundabout way of attempting to meet some need. Focus on uncovering the need and meeting it, or showing the kid how they can meet it, rather than getting distracted by the attempted manipulation.

If manipulative behavior becomes a pattern—a particular kid having problem after problem that I'm pretty sure are all made up—I might say, "You know, Tom, I've noticed that a lot of things have come up for you that make this trip difficult—trouble with your ankle, headaches, difficulty setting up your tent—and I'm wondering if those are really the problems or if there's something else going on? You seem like a pretty healthy, capable person to me. I want you to know that I'm here to support you in whatever you need. If you need something, you can come to me, whether you have a headache or not."

Kids came up with problems all the time. As much as I wanted to be supportive and offer my help when kids genuinely had problems, I didn't want them to get the idea they could run me around in circles with their made-up difficulties 24-7. Here are some ways I demonstrated that:

Delay: "It sounds to me like this is something that can wait until tomorrow, when we're all rested. It's been a long day, come to me about it tomorrow if it's still a problem."

Defer to the Group: "This sounds like a great thing to bring up in the next Group, so we can all support you in it." (i.e. so there's transparency and I'm not the only one who will have to respond to your made-up problems). Kids generally won't take up the group's time to talk about made-up problems.

Humor: In the field there are limited things we can do to respond to physical or medical ailments, so I found myself frequently replying to kids' problems with the number one solution in the backcountry: drink water.

"Mark, I have a headache."

"Drink water."

"Mark, I feel tired."

"Drink water."

"I feel nauseous."

"Did you drink enough water?"

"I haven't used the latrine all expedition."

"Drink more water!"

Water really does help with each of the above things. Often kids simply don't bother to dig out their water bottle from their pack during rest breaks. Or they may be unused to high altitude, or the intense exercise of backpacking. So I was addressing their needs. However, given how often I found myself saying "just drink water," I made it into a running joke:

"Mark, I can't figure out how to set up my tent."

"Drink more water."

"Tracy's getting on my nerves!"

"Drink half a bottle of cold water followed by a quarter bottle of lukewarm water."

"What do I need to do to get you to take me seriously?"

"Drink more water, way more water!"

Humor is a great way to jostle the brain out of a stuck mentality and have a bit of fun while doing it. If ten minutes later the student is still having trouble with their tent, or annoyed at Tracy, or wanting me to take them seriously, then I'll come over and help.

Give them something, anything, to do that is within their control: Often kids' emotional experiences manifest in physical ways, given the physical challenges of hiking and backpacking in the wilderness. This is another benefit of Wilderness Therapy, the physical challenges can bring forth emotional challenges in a safe environment where they can be worked through, rather than waiting for them to come up in a crisis point in life where there may not be support. When psychosomatic symptoms come up, the kid really experiences them as physical. This isn't an attempt at manipulation. But in terms of how I responded, the distinction didn't matter, because the response was still to find a solution. I gave kids plausible physical cures that were entirely within their control (even if those cures had a flimsy medical basis). "Step this way when you hike," "Hold your backpack straps like this to open up your lungs," and of course, "Drink water." Telling kids to "drink water" is a very effective placebo out in the field, and one that they can continue to use easily, on their own, for the rest of their lives. This is a simple way to give kids a direct experience of having more control over their own well-being, a way for them to develop more self-sufficiency. These experiences—examples of what they know they're capable of—will serve as resources later in life when crises arise.

46.

Roles

Get used to stepping into different roles. We all have different roles we play depending on the context we find ourselves in: friend, boss, employee, husband, wife, leader, follower, etc. We step into most of these roles unconsciously based on the context we find ourselves in. However, it is useful to expand the roles we are able to step into, and to be conscious and flexible about *what* role we step into *when*. Without this flexibility, we may miss opportunities, or step into roles that are counter-productive.

Have you ever been in a situation where everyone was in the same role—too many cooks in the kitchen? Usually it doesn't work very well. During my college wilderness leadership course we each had an opportunity to practice leading our group composed entirely of people who wanted to be wilderness trip leaders. It was interesting practice, and became difficult when some of us forgot to stay in follower mode on days when we weren't leading (which, as you can imagine, happened a lot). That experience of leading other leaders, was in some ways more challenging than leading an ordinary group of people who will tend to settle into complimentary roles.

If you are flexible in what role you are able to step into, you will have more influence than someone who doesn't have that choice. Again, all else being equal, the element in the system with the most flexibility, will have the most influence. (See tool 32, "If it isn't working, try something else," page 154.) Other than my "group leader" role, here are other roles I stepped into:

Follower: Turning over responsibility to one kid to be the Leader of the Day, and deferring to them when any questions were directed towards me about the hike length, direction, water breaks, time to camp, etc.

Mentor: Supporting students in discovering what their passions/ goals are.

King: Exaggerating my position of leadership over my "subjects" making "decrees" etc.

Teacher: Teaching specific wilderness or communication skills, such as map reading, Nonviolent Communication, how to light a stove, wilderness medicine, etc.

Kid: Taking the same position as a student, such as when they complained about the program, I would complain about it *with* them even more than they were complaining.

Friend: Joking around and having fun connecting as an equal.

Criminal: Seeing how long the students would buy my story of operating outside the law (A way of joining with the kids who often *were* criminals according to the law, or were treated like criminals).

Father: Modeling what a *supportive* father does (providing for them unconditionally, etc.). I never used the word "father," which will tend to have lots of negative triggers for these kids who are mostly in a troubled relationship with their parents.

Holder of Sacred Space: Acknowledging the spiritual or metaphysical side of things, no matter someone's religion or lack thereof. Providing and honoring space for reflection and introspection.

Clown: Entertaining and joking around.

Counselor/Therapist: Coaching and counseling the kids as they work through their personal growth process.

Master of Games: Creating and leading fun games and play.

Of course there are many more roles than what I've listed. Find your own roles, play with them, continue to expand the list. This will give you great freedom and open up all kinds of possibilities.

47.

Keep relationships clean

When you have a rocky relationship with a student, it's worth keeping all interactions squeaky clean. For example one trip I ran out of my prized commodity of cheese a few nights early. I was commenting on how much better my beans and rice would taste with some cheese, when Jason said, "I have extra cheese, you can have some of mine." Now if this was a student with whom I had a perfectly fine relationship, and they really did have more than they were going to eat, that would be one thing. But Jason and I had a rocky relationship. An offer like this may seem like a pretty harmless thing, even a chance to connect with a student that has been giving you trouble. Think again.

I never wanted these difficult students in a position of power over my well-being, even for a moment in the form of cheese. If I accepted the gift of cheese, Jason could easily see me as in his debt, and I didn't want that. This is why we never allow any trading or bartering of any kind between students. You'd be amazed how prized one bite of bagel can become towards the end of an expedition. I heard stories of girls trading sexual favors for food.

Once one of my co-instructors made the mistake of accepting a gift of a bagel from a student. He probably figured that accepting the gift from Jenny could be a positive acknowledgement of Jenny doing something positive for him (of which, up until that point, there were very few examples). Later, when my co-instructor asked Jenny not to have a private conversation with another girl, Jenny said, "I think we really could use some space. I don't think it's too much to ask. I respect you and even gave you a bagel last night, can't you return the favor and just give us a little space to connect?" By accepting the bagel the night before, my co-instructor had made his job twice as hard. Now, he not only had the task of making it clear why private conversations have no place at Monarch, but also the task of separating Jenny's "generosity" the night before from the issue of not allowing private conversations.

"Jenny," he said. "Last night you told me you weren't going to eat your bagel. I appreciated your generosity last night, and accepted that gift as a gift, not as a trade for you being able to break a Monarch rule.

"Well you broke a Monarch rule by sharing my bagel, isn't there a rule of no sharing?"

"There's a rule of no sharing between students, staff are different."

"Then you can make this different."

You can see how this has gotten completely side-tracked from the simple issue of setting a clear boundary (no private conversations). It's much harder to separate two issues that have been conflated by a student, than to just make sure they stay separate, clean, and clear from the beginning. By accepting the bagel the night before, my co-instructor set the stage for these two separate things to become joined. More important, this made it more difficult for Jenny to learn how to have a healthy, clear, and clean relationship. This is the real reason I never accepted these gifts or offerings from kids—it confused *them*, making it more difficult for them to learn, through experience, what a healthy relationship looks like and feels like.

If there's a rule between the kids, (such as "no sharing, borrowing, or lending") it will be much easier for them to learn and abide by it if you model it yourself. If you are going to have a different rule apply to you than the one that applies to the kids, then have a good reason for it, not just that you'd really enjoy a bagel that night.

So when Jason said, "I have extra cheese, you can have some of mine." I replied, "No thanks, Jason, "I really appreciate the offer. As much as it would taste good, I don't want to take any of your share of cheese, and maybe a few nights without cheese will be good for me. It's good for us all to take a few nights off and re-examine our addictions."

"I'm not gonna eat it anyway," Jason persisted.

"Who knows what the future holds. Maybe we'll get lost out here and then you'll be glad I turned down your generous offer."

So be aware of anything like this that could be used later as a basis for manipulation, or create confusion about your relationship. The cheese really isn't worth the extra hassle it's likely to cause. Keep it simple and clean: You are here to provide for them and keep them safe, and in return you need and ask for absolutely nothing.

48.

The wilderness as teacher

Nowhere do natural and logical consequences speak more strongly than in the wilderness, where a storm can move in at any time, an animal can get the food that wasn't properly hung, and a fire is only as good as the time spent building and tending it. Group dynamics are also clear to see during group tasks such as hiking, cooking meals in the same pot, working together to hang food in a tree, or digging one latrine where everyone shits.

So what else does the wilderness teach?

For me, learning about and understanding the natural world has given me a great respect for the fact that we literally cannot survive as a species without it. We rely completely on the natural world to give us food and provide us with a huge part of our shelter, heat, transportation, and technology. We also rely on the ability of the natural world to absorb and offset the pollution that our society pumps into the environment every day.

Learning about ecological systems teaches about the complexity and interrelatedness of all things. Upsetting one aspect of an ecosystem can have unintended consequences that cascade through the system. It's important to honor all aspects of an ecosystem, and how the system as a whole works together. This can be a powerful metaphor for ourselves; it's important to honor all parts of ourselves as well. There may be parts we "don't like," but trying to eliminate that part will be difficult, make the whole eco-system less rich, and likely have unintended negative consequences if we succeed.

In one area we backpacked in the Rocky Mountains, the pine beetle was in the process of killing entire mountainsides of pine trees. Some students asked about the "red pines," that from a distance looked rather pretty, even though they were red because they were dried out and dead. So I taught the kids on that trip about how communities all over the Rocky Mountains began fighting forest fires to protect themselves and their homes. What they didn't know is that the ecosystem had evolved with forest fires that would start naturally as a result of lightning strikes. These fires would burn up grass and dead wood and weak trees, returning their nutrients to the ground, creating space for new plant life to grow. Because the fires happened regularly, they rarely got hot enough to burn large established trees, but simply cleared out the undergrowth for a healthy forest, creating space for new saplings to take root. When people started preventing these fires, the dead grass and wood started to build up, and the forests became choked with lots of medium-sized trees competing with each other for resources. None of the trees had room to grow big and healthy, and no smaller trees had enough light or space to get started. These medium-sized unhealthy forests were very vulnerable to the pine beetle, which kills the weaker trees that it bores into, and whole mountainsides died off. The dense unhealthy forests and years of accumulated wood also became a huge fire hazard like nothing the Rocky Mountains had ever seen before. When these mountainsides caught fire, they burned out of control of even the best fire-fighting teams. And rather than burning in a healthy way, clearing out the dead wood and weaker trees, *everything* burned. The fires even burned so hot they scorched the topsoil, robbing it of its precious organic nutrients. Much of this depleted, scorched soil would then be lost to wind and water erosion with no living plants left to hold it on the slopes. Revegetation and reforestation was a long and slow process after one of these fires.

Just as with an evolving eco-system, during our personal evolution it is important to make sure that any change in ourselves works well with our whole ecology of self (as well as with the larger ecology of our relationships and place in society as a whole). It is easy to think we can just suppress parts of ourselves that we don't like, just like mountain communities tried to suppress all forest fires, but often this leads to increased damage further on down the line. A better solution is to understand that there are positives to every aspect of our behavior, just as there are positives to every aspect of an ecosystem. When we recognize that every aspect of ourselves has some positive role to play for our whole being, we can look for the right balance rather than trying to completely suppress or eliminate a part of ourselves that we don't like, only to have it come back later with even greater force. Communities in the Rocky Mountains now have proscribed burns, and other fire mitigation efforts, so that the ecosystem can have the fires it needs in order to be healthy, in a way that also protects people and homes.

The natural world also offers the most abundant array of powerful metaphors for healing and growth. Everywhere you look in the wilderness, things are alive and growing and thriving even in the most difficult habitats of desert or alpine tundra. Seeing and experiencing all this growth around us can be a constant unconscious reminder that we are a part of that growth and ability to survive and thrive no matter where we find ourselves.

To read a story of a woman who overcame cancer after paying attention to her internal ecology, see the story "Internal Garden" near the end of my book *Sweet Fruit from the Bitter Tree: 61 stories of creative and compassionate ways out of conflict.*

The wilderness setting also offers the experience of a tangible, obvious, and immediate sense of accomplishment due to what I've done with my own two hands and my own two feet: "I climbed this mountain," "I started this fire," "I cooked this meal," "I read this map," "I led this group." A backpacking wilderness trip provides a powerful, real experience of not just surviving, but *thriving* with nothing more than what you can carry with you: "I hiked this hike with everything I need right here on my back!"

I'm not a very spiritual person, but even I have a sense of spiritual awe when I have the privilege of witnessing a night full of meteors, a bull moose with water plants dangling from his mouth, a vast sunset lit up across the entire sky, a lightning storm crashing all around me, the perfect reflection of a mountain lake, a bear lumbering away through the woods, a bat clinging to a tree where a piece of bark fell away, the vista from a 14,000 ft. peak, or the unique character of each glacier-carved alpine valley. And all of this, I believe, has value beyond my ability to put down in words.

SECTION III: Further Tales

Chapter Four

The Wall*

We were in the middle of a trip in Rocky Mountain National Park and my group of eight adolescent boys had just finished a weekend of therapy. The therapists had left the field that morning and my co-instructor, Molly, and I started out with our group on the beginning of a six-mile hike to our next camp. The morning sun slanted through the thinning pines, illuminating the steep slopes of the valley as we ascended through the cliffs onto a plateau above tree line.

We had only been underway ten minutes when one of the guys started lagging behind.

"Hold on up there!" I shouted to the kids in front, and they waited for Travis to catch up.

---

* This story first appeared in my book *Sweet Fruit from the Bitter Tree: 61 stories of creative and compassionate ways out of conflict*, a collection of true accounts, from a wide variety of contributors, of how ordinary people found extraordinary and useful solutions to all manner of life conflicts. Available on Amazon.com.

"We need to keep the group together," I said when Travis caught up with the rest of the bunch.

One of the other boys came back to talk to him. Jordan was a super athlete—a competitive skier with the strong muscular build of a wrestler. Frustration showed in his eyes to be slowed down this early in the day. "Hey Travis," Jordan said, "Will you walk up front so we can keep the group together? I don't like stopping and starting all the time."

Travis looked at the ground, also frustrated. He didn't respond.

"Travis, will you go to the front?!"

"Travis," I asked, "Will you respond to Jordan's request?" He just shook his head. "Can you at least tell Jordan you need space right now?" Nothing. "God damn it!" Jordan cursed. After a bit more trying it was clear that Travis wasn't going to engage.

"Jordan, he's obviously not in a space to talk about it right now. I appreciate you asking him respectfully, and I wish he could respect you by responding. That's clearly not going to happen right now, so let's keep hiking."

"Fuck! Why won't you just go to the fucking front?!" Jordan stormed to the front of the trail. "It's bitches like you that make this take all day. I just want to get to fucking camp!"

In minutes the group was spread out again and we had to stop for Travis a second time. Tensions were rising with Jordan and some of the other boys, and the cursing and angry comments increased.

My co-instructor Molly said, "Jordan, I agree with you that Travis is acting inappropriately right now, and that's no reason for you to do the same by calling him names behind his back." But when we got going again the sideways remarks continued.

"It looks to me like you guys want to have Group," I said.

"No, you've gotta be kidding," Jordan said.

"Well, you obviously have a lot to say, so let's have a Group and talk about it. What do you think Molly? How about up on the plateau behind those rocks."

"I think that sounds like an excellent plan."

"You've gotta be kidding," Jordan repeated, shaking his head. "I'm not having Group."

At the top of the plateau the rest of the kids stopped, but Jordan kept powering ahead. "Have a nice Group," he said. "I'll see you in camp."

Molly stayed with the seven kids while I dropped my pack and ran after Jordan as he disappeared over a hill. I jogged past him and stood in front of him, blocking his way forward on the trail. My heart was pounding from more than just the jog. I remembered a few weeks earlier when Jordan had destroyed several aspen saplings in a rage because of what he saw as an unjust consequence.

"We need to keep the group together, Jordan." I said.

"I'm not going back there. I'll see you at fucking camp." He took one step off the path and I mirrored his movement to block his way forward. Then he stepped off in the other direction and I mirrored him again.

"We can't let you go on alone, Jordan. If something happens to you we're responsible."

"Nothing will happen."

"We can't know that."

"Will you restrain me?"

"Maybe," I said. What he didn't know was that we weren't allowed to restrain a kid unless two people were present, and with a kid Jordan's build we probably wouldn't even try a two-person take down.

"Jordan, I don't want to get into a struggle with you." I kept talking, hoping to keep him from trying to solve his problem physically. "I just want to keep the group together and safe. Let's go back, you can leave your pack here and we'll pick it up when we continue hiking."

"If I go back there now I'll look like an idiot."

"I think the group might appreciate you coming back."

Jordan shook his head.

"You're kind of stuck, aren't you? Go forward and you have to deal with me, go back and you'll feel like you lost."

"Yep." He bit off the word sharply, still paused in indecision with one foot off the trail. I waited for a bit, but nothing changed, so I decided to try a different tack.

"I can see you're pretty upset," I said. "What's going on for you right now?"

"I want to get to fucking camp."

"Jordan, I know you want to get to camp, but there's more to it than that. What's triggering you so much about this."

He just shook his head.

"I'd really like to know what's going on, but I feel like you've got this big wall up."

"Yep," he said with a defiant glint in his eye. "I'm balancing on that wall right now and I don't know which way I'll fall."

"Which way would you like to fall?

"I think I'll just keep walking until it gets thinner and thinner and I'll be forced to fall."

I took a breath. Jordan was a smart kid. We could trade metaphors all day without making any progress. Our conversation lapsed into silence as we stood there in a standoff. I was out of ideas.

I glanced down at the gold cross hanging on a chain around his neck. Well, if we were going to stand here for a while I might as well learn something.

"Where'd you get that cross?" I asked.

"My uncle gave it to me. He got it on a trip to Spain. It's real gold."

"That's cool. My dad used to bring me back old coins when he went traveling."

"Were they gold?"

"He found a gold coin on an airplane once. It was about that big," I indicated a circle with my finger and thumb. "But he found the owner. It was probably worth about fifty bucks. The ones he brought back to me were silver though. They were old Greek coins. One has the Pegasus on it—the flying horse. They're not even round; they were made so long ago they're all lopsided, and sometimes the printed circle goes off the edge of the coin. They're pretty neat."

Jordan shifted his weight. "Alright, I'll go back but I'm not saying anything."

"That's fine. You can leave your backpack here if you want."

"I'll just leave it on."

"OK."

Jordan turned back down the trail and I followed him back to the group. It wasn't any clever strategy that worked. By simply connecting with him in a different realm, I was no longer in opposition to him. Instead I was another person who had received something special from a family member. That connection invited him away from the wall where there were no good solutions.

Chapter Five

Damage Control

At the end of one of our out-of-state expeditions, one of the kids went completely defiant. He'd screwed up, which meant he knew he wasn't going to earn time with his family when we got home, and in his mind he was sure that he'd get pulled from Monarch and sent to a lock-down facility. Being good had no benefit to him, so he decided he might as well be bad.

In the middle of our 2-day drive back to Colorado, we camped overnight in Oklahoma. When I did the nightly round to check on the kids before bed and make sure they were all in their tents, I smelled burning tobacco near Tucker's tent.

"Tucker, are you smoking in there?" I asked.

"Yeah."

I opened his tent fly and looked inside to see that he was smoking an old half-used cigarette he'd found. In his other hand was a lighter.

"Where'd you get the lighter?" I asked.

"I found it."

"Can I see it?"

To my surprise, he tossed it to me. "Can I have the cigarette as well."

"No. Give me back the lighter."

"Tucker, you know that lighters and cigarettes aren't student items while at Monarch. I'm going to hold on to the lighter." I didn't make an issue of the cigarette, which he knew (and I made clear again by stating it), that he wasn't supposed to have.

As I looked at Tucker smoking defiantly in his tent, I considered what to do next. In the past several days I'd already had countless conversations with him about his future, about the best choices he could make to have the future he wanted, and how I was here to support him in getting the life that he wanted for himself. Right now it was late and time for bed.

"Good night, Tucker," I said, zipping up his tent fly and walking back to my tent. I got inside my sleeping bag and closed my eyes, letting everything go for the time being so that I could get some sleep.

The next day we packed up camp and started our final day of driving. As we crossed the border into Kansas Tucker slid even farther, piercing me with a constant glare every time we stopped for gas, or when I looked in the rear view mirror. My co-instructor, Jessica, felt utterly unsafe around him, so I let her drive and I sat directly behind her so none of the kids could interfere with her driving.

"Hey, fish-face!" Tucker sneered at me. "Yeah Mark, I'm talking to *you*, fish-face! Look at him, he's always gulping like a fish!"

"Tucker, I know you're in a rough place right now, and I'm sorry about that," I said.

"Whatever, fish face!" Tucker sneered again.

"My mother was in fact a fish," I said.

"Probably why you look so much like a fucking fish!"

I tried empathy, I tried humor, I tried ignoring, I tried every trick I could think of in this book. Nothing worked. At this point my job was containment. The best thing I could do was make sure the rest of the group stayed safe and that they didn't get pulled into any bad dynamic with Tucker, either by joining him or picking a fight with him. In eight hours we would be back in Georgetown with the full support of the rest of the Monarch staff. My job was to keep things from getting physical between now and then.

"I have a request of the rest of the group," I said.

"Fish face has a request!" Tucker sneered.

I nodded to Tucker and continued speaking to the group. "If we need to, we will stop and have a Group or do whatever we need so that everyone here feels comfortable with the drive back. Obviously Tucker isn't in contact right now, so my request of all of you is that you don't engage with him until he's ready to be in contact again. Is that agreeable to everyone here?"

Everyone nodded. To be very thorough, I asked each kid individually, waiting for their verbal and nonverbal response, watching for any signs that a kid might feel threatened by Tucker, or be tempted to fight or join him. They all looked and sounded congruent in their verbal agreements with me.

"OK, thank you," I said to the group, "If you change your mind that's fine, just let me know so we can stop and work things out. Is everyone comfortable with where they are sitting? If anyone would like more space away from Tucker we can arrange that."

Everyone was OK as is; Tucker wasn't focusing his negativity on any of the other kids, just on me.

"I know that being cramped in a van doesn't help anything," I continued, "and I also want to be very clear that Tucker's behavior won't have any effect on each of your family time when we get back to Georgetown. Tucker's decisions affect his time with his family, and your decisions affect your time. As long as you all stay disengaged from Tucker, you'll have the time you've earned with your family."

I did everything I could to ensure that the group was with me, and I could see that they were. With Tucker my only goal at this point was containment, to keep him from getting violent.

As the ride continued and Tucker kept showering me with abuse, I felt my muscles tighten and I grew more and more tense under the constant verbal attacks. As the hours stretched on, I kept my arm on the back of the seat so that Tucker's actions never left my peripheral vision. I was on the lookout for any signs that he might get physical, and if that happened I would call the police.

Finally we arrived back in Georgetown after what seemed like the longest van ride of my life. We stopped to fill up the van with gas one last time and the kids got out to use the bathroom. Tucker found some half-burned cigarettes in an ashtray outside the gas station and asked a nearby smoker for a light. There was no point in my trying to stop him.

I walked up to Tucker and said, "So this is the choice you're making."

"Yep," he blew cigarette smoke straight in my face. I took a step back, and finally I felt all the tension drain out of me. My mission was accomplished, we were back in Georgetown, and this was my last night. If I needed to I could just call the cops and drive away tomorrow. Or maybe, despite my best efforts, there had still been a part of me that got hooked by Tucker—that had felt I needed to control the situation—and only now could I realize that and let it go. In this moment with Tucker I recognized that there was a part of me that felt betrayed by him. We'd made such a great connection on my previous expedition; how could he just forget all that and treat me this way?

That might have been a useful question if Tucker were my peer, but Tucker wasn't my peer. When I recognized this in myself I could fully let go of the power control battle I'd been on the verge of getting into all day with Tucker. I could finally let down my guard, a fake protection that did nothing but give Tucker something solid to push against.

"Tucker," I said. "I think you're a really cool guy, and I just want you to know that I really valued our connection on the first expedition. I want the best for you. I felt sad this expedition when you gave up on graduating from Monarch. I also felt sad when you called me names on the ride up here, because I really enjoyed connecting with you about your fantasy writing, and chess and all the things we found in common last expedition. I apologize for any screw-ups I made on this expedition. I'm sure there were things I could have handled better. Anyway I just want you to know that it's hard for me to see you give up and assume you're just going to end up in a lock-down facility. I hope there are other options for you, and no matter how hard things get, I'm still here to support you in finding another way if you decide you want to."

Chapter Six

Teenager Außer Kontrolle

I had officially left my job as a full-time field instructor, but then I got a call from Monarch asking me if I wanted to be on one of the biggest German Reality Television shows, "*Teenager* außer Kontrolle," (Teenagers out of Control). Six teenagers were being flown from Germany to go through the Monarch program for several months before flying back.

I have a personal dislike of reality TV shows in general, and based on the ones I'd seen, the shows are premised on putting people in situations that *create* drama and conflict, as opposed to resolving it. So I was very curious to find out whether or not I would find this job objectionable.

As it was, on the whole I was very impressed with the film crew. They were respectful people, and at least one of them was genuinely interested in conflict resolution. They described themselves as a cross between reality show and documentary. Obviously they needed to show the conflict that kids started out with, but their goal was to show the program working for the kids over the course of their time in the program. And I couldn't argue with the fact that the show paid the way for every student.

I didn't end up on film very much. Since I don't speak German, I wasn't being hired as a field instructor, but rather a trainer of the field instructors, and a coordinator between the field instructors, the camera crew, and the therapists. Monarch ended up with an interesting combination of field instructors to lead the German kids. Thomas had been brought over from Germany, spoke fluent German, and had no clue how to lead. Deena had a good grasp of leadership, but spoke almost no German. Rickard spoke fluent German and English, so the bulk of the leadership naturally ended up on his shoulders, and he was often stuck in the role of translator. All three of them had never led a wilderness therapy group before, and every moment of it was going to be filmed.

Because the leaders were all so new, during the wilderness portion of the trip I ended up taking over a lot of the leadership role along with my colleague Rachel, who had also been hired in the same role as I.

On our second day of hiking we had a long way to go, and it was important for us to make it to our planned campsite because the next day was going to be longer—12 miles with no water along the way. But the new field staff did not take charge of pacing. They let short breaks stretch on for fifteen or twenty minutes. When Rachel and I advised the staff to get the group moving, they'd tell the group, "All right, we need to get going now." But when the kids ignored them, the field staff weren't persistent, and Thomas didn't even pick his own butt off the ground.

So after most of the morning wasted away, Rachel and I just took over leadership of the group. We kept breaks short, kept the group moving, stopped to make dinner before dark, then hiked some more. One or two of the kids spoke pretty good English, and they told me that they didn't like some things their leaders were doing, specifically Rickard. A lot of pressure was being put on Rickard because Thomas was useless for all I could tell, and Deena spoke basically no German.

"What didn't you like that Rickard did?" I asked.

"He's too demanding, he doesn't respect us when he tells us what to do."

"What makes you think he doesn't respect you?"

"He just tells us sharply to do stuff, and doesn't care about anything else."

"Well I'm sorry you felt that way. I'd be happy to talk with you and him about it if you want…"

It's interesting how much is revealed when a group of teens actually goes backpacking, not just camping but carrying everything with them on their own back, making a new camp each night with the same people and the same basic supplies. I could feel the whole group getting restless. The earlier portion of the trip they'd been camping at a base camp at the sand dunes, and after this backpacking portion of the trip, they'd once again be base-camped at a wolf sanctuary and then on an Indian reservation—all wonderful opportunities, but complicated by contact with a wider range of other people, and not nearly as difficult. This backpacking portion would be by far the most challenging, and every learning experience that came up in the group would be painted clearly on the pristine canvass of the wilderness, not lost in the chaos of society.

As dark descended, Rachel and I led the group as far as we could before we set up our tents on a ridge and went to sleep.

The next day the group was bickering and complaining, taking a long time to get tents packed up. This was not a good way to start our longest and most challenging day, in fact, one of the longest most challenging hikes I ever led at Monarch. We'd been granted access to cross private land, but had no permission to camp there, and once we got back on public land there would be no water until camp. All in all it would be 12 miles of hiking, about twice the distance we'd barely managed the day before, and all without the benefit of a trail. We had to start this day off right, or we'd never make it. Failing the hike would have been the easy way out, and both Rachel and I felt strongly that we'd be letting these kids down if we didn't give them success for the one wilderness portion of their time in a Wilderness Therapy program.

Because the official field instructors were out of their depth, both in leading the group and in navigating off-trail to our next camp site, we all agreed that Rachel and I would lead today as well. But I knew that if this group was going to make it, I had to do a lot more than get an early start on the day. When we were ready to hike, we gathered the group together in a circle and I asked Rickard to translate for me as the camera man video-recorded everyone but me and Rachel.

"I notice that there's been a lot of bickering, arguing, and complaining that started yesterday evening and hasn't stopped this morning." I paused for Rickard to translate. "I know that this is very different for you, that this is hard work, and that when we're living in this close proximity to each other, it can be easy to get on each other's nerves." Every sentence or two I'd pause again for Rickard, but even though he was translating, I didn't speak to him. I looked each teen in the eye as I spoke, and as Rickard spoke. "What I want to be very clear on," I said, "is that I am here to support you and make this hike go the best that it possibly can for everyone. So if you have some problem with anything, come straight to me, or to Rachel or Rickard or Thomas or Deena. If something's not working for you, let us know so that we can fix it. Is that something all of you can do?"

I was always careful to get feedback from teens I talked to. Here they all nodded, so I went on. "We have a big hike ahead of us today. It won't be easy, but if we all work together, I have no doubt that we'll accomplish it. Now, I'm sure you all have noticed a lot more bickering and arguments in the group this morning—a lot more than usual. After today, we'll have plenty of time to have a Group to talk over any concerns that any of you may have, either between each other, or between you and a staff member. But today we don't have time for that if we all want to get into camp before dark, and I think we would all like to get in before dark, am I right?"

Again the students nodded. "Great. Thank you. I appreciate that you all are willing to wait, and we will have time to have a

Group about anything you want once we get through this hike. I want you all to know we have a big hike ahead of us today, quite a bit longer than yesterday. During the first half we'll be going through private property, where we're not allowed to stay over-night. During the second half of the hike there will be no water at all until we get into camp. So it's important that we make good time. There's no trail the whole way; that will make the trip take longer than if there was a trail. Are there any questions about the hike?"

Rickard translated the questions from students, which I answered. Then I continued.

"As I already said, I noticed a lot of bickering and arguing this morning and yesterday evening. Now it's easy to get on each other's nerves when we're this close together without much of a break, without time to just be quiet by ourselves or have per-sonal time. For safety, it's important that we all stick together, but even when we're together there are ways that we can have personal time and quiet time. So that's what I ask we do for this morning's hike. I ask that we all hike in complete silence.

"Now, some of you may not like it, others of you will. But as we hike in silence this morning I want you to just notice what you like or dislike about hiking in silence. What do you notice? And how is it different than hiking when everyone is talking? Is this something everyone can agree to?"

Most of the kids nodded, but one girl had her arms crossed and her eyes averted.

"Does anyone have any objections to starting the hike off in silence?" I asked.

No one spoke up with any objection, but the girl kept her eyes downcast and her arms folded across her chest, her body language speaking far louder than words.

"Krista," I said, "when you do this," I mirrored her stance with crossed arms and downcast gaze, "I get the idea that you don't agree with what I'm saying. Do you need something?"

She uncrossed her arms and shook her head, glancing up at me and looking away.

"Will you meet my eyes and make contact?" I asked.

Rickard translated and she looked up at me. "Thank you, Krista," I said. "Is there anything you need before you feel comfortable starting the hike in silence?" I wanted to be very thorough here, going a little slower now to save lots of time later.

Krista shook her head.

"If that ever changes and you decide you need something, will you come straight to me?" I asked.

She responded in German. "Sure, she will," Rickard translated back to me.

"Thank you," I said.

I looked up at the whole group.

"That goes for all of you," I said. "If any of you have anything at all that you need, come straight to me or one of the other leaders so we can fix it."

"OK, we're going to begin hiking in silence now. We'll probably hike in silence for about an hour, maybe longer. I'll let everyone know when it's time to speak again."

I asked Rickard to lead the hike, because it was key that the kids see him in a position of leadership, (given he was the only capable field instructor who also spoke German). I spaced out Thomas, Deena, Rachel, and myself through the hiking order every couple kids to further ensure that silence was observed. With nothing to say, we all just hiked, and we made great time. I know that for myself it was a hugely welcome silence.

When we had to stop for a water break, I would stop, get out my water bottle, and motion the kids to do the same, still maintaining silence. In keeping silent suddenly the kids had to use different senses, shifting from predominately talking *about* experience, mostly past or future (auditory digital), to much more visual, auditory, and kinesthetic present-moment experiencing. Suddenly there was the time and space for each student to *feel* the ground underfoot and the cool air on their faces, to *see* the sunbeams lancing through the pine boughs, and to *hear* the creaking of our backpacks and the chirping of the birds in the distance. Students were free not only to notice their surroundings, but also to take in each other's body language, or just have time with their own thoughts.

Because I had been very thorough with the pre-framing of what we were doing, taking time to make sure all objections were settled before we started, not a single student spoke a word during the silent hike. After about an hour we felt like a completely different group. I asked them each to take 5 or 10 minutes to journal on what they'd noticed, and whether they'd liked it or disliked it. Then we gathered everyone in a circle and had a group conversation about what we'd each noticed during the silence.

I don't remember a single student who didn't appreciate the silence, and how well the group worked together.

As we started up again, I said that anyone could talk now, who wanted to, but of course you don't have to either, if you don't want to. We had a very tranquil and pleasant day of hiking, despite the students being pushed to the max. Darkness fell as we arrived at the road along which we were supposed to find our water source. The other leaders and I got out our headlamps, and we all continued down the road. I was mentally noting the dirty puddles we passed in case the spring was dried up. Those puddles could be used as a water source in a pinch. Finally we decided to make camp, though we still hadn't come to any spring. The exhausted kids climbed straight into their tents. None of them even cared about food, but Rachel and I made them each a half bagel with tuna fish, which they ate gratefully, drinking the last of their water before falling fast asleep.

The next day we packed up and found our water source just a little ways on down the road, where we stopped for a nice hot breakfast of grits, celebrating their huge accomplishment the day before.

Chapter Seven

How to deal with "@#$%#! impossible parents!!"

He sat stewing in the passenger seat as I drove him to the airport, a deep frown on his face. Robbie was on his way home after more than two months at Monarch, though I had only met him the day before.

He shook his head, scowling. "My dad's such an ass. He's always like this. It's not gonna work back at home. I'm just gonna get thrown out of the house. He's giving me no choice. So much for college!"

After working two years as a year-round wilderness therapy instructor, I had officially quit to start an individual private practice. But I still found myself unable to resist returning to cover for a day or two now and then. This was one of those days.

Robbie set down the list of "Rules for Home" that he had just finished reading. I was a little taken aback by Robbie's situation. Robbie had been here a long time. Now he was going home. I thought he was a great kid. Were the last two months for nothing?

"I'm sorry," I said. "Sounds like you got a few surprises in there? Did you talk about any of this in your last therapy session with your parents?"

"No, I spent most of it outside the room. My parents have a lot of issues to work out."

"Wow, that must have been frustrating having hardly any time to talk about your needs."

"Yeah, it's all right."

"So tell me about these rules for home that you just read."

"It pisses me off, my dad's always just laying down ultimatums."

"I'd be pissed off too, if I spent two months in a program and didn't get any input into the rules for going home."

"Yeah."

We talked a bit more about what he'd read, and I heard him out as he told me his point of view. I asked him what his goals were for home. Going to college was a big one, which wasn't going to be easy on his own if he had to get a job and pay rent. He wanted to finish High School to get to college, which wasn't going to be easy on his own either, but if he didn't abide by his dad's rules he was going to be kicked out of the house.

"So you have one more year of high school," I observed. "Do you think it would be worth it to put up with the rules for this last year, so you can go to college like you want?"

"Maybe."

"So of all these rules, even if none of them is ideal, which are going to be the hardest for you? Let's say you decide to go along with these rules for your own goals—of going to college and having the benefits of a place to sleep and food on the table, and anything else your parents can support you in. As annoying as the rules will be sometimes, which of them will be hardest for you to deal with?"

After talking it over and getting a chance to have his point of view heard, Robbie realized he was actually OK with most of the rules. Putting myself in his position, I imagined that much of his objection to them was simply that he hadn't been consulted.

Once I heard his point of view, there was really no problem with most of the rules themselves.

But there were still three that were going to be hard: Not being able to play his music, eating dinner with his parents five days a week, and not smoking pot.

"Great, now which of those three is the least difficult?" I asked.

"The music."

"So why don't they let you play your music?"

"They say it's too loud for the neighbors."

"Oh, so if you could do it in a way that didn't disturb the neighbors would they be OK with it?"

"I guess."

"Do you have any ideas how you could meet your parents needs and still be able to listen to music?"

"I guess I could stuff clothes in the vents. I did try that once."

"Did it work?"

"I don't think my parents knew about it."

"Oh, so maybe that would be something to check with them and see if it made it quiet enough for them. What about an iPod?"

"I don't have the money to get one."

"Maybe that's something your parents would be willing to help you buy as long as you were doing well in school, and respecting the boundaries they've set for you? Have you asked them about that?"

"No."

"Do you think they'd be up for it?"

"Yeah, probably."

"Great. Here's something you can learn about your parents that could really help you out. There will probably be other times when they'll set a limit with you, tell you "no this" or "no that." It's annoying right? If you can figure out what they really want, then you have a chance at coming to a solution that works for both you and your parents. In this case they didn't really want you to stop listening to music. What they wanted was to avoid upsetting the neighbors. There are lots of ways to listen to music and not piss off your neighbors."

"Yeah, you're right."

"So how are you with that rule now?"

"Better, I think I can work that out now."

"Let me know if there are still problems, so we can talk about it and find a way that works for you and your goals."

"No, I think I'm good with that one."

"OK, so which of the remaining two is less difficult: not smoking pot, or eating sit-down dinners with your parents?"

"I guess eating dinner with my parents, but there's just no way that's happening."

"Well let's just say you decided to do it, what would be the hardest part?"

"Ughh! It would just be too awkward. We never eat dinner together."

"So, I understand that it might just be really awkward at first. Can you think of anything that would make it less awkward?"

"Well, I guess if they agreed to let me cook them dinner at least once a week."

His answer took me completely by surprise. I was glad I'd asked him for a solution. I wouldn't have come up with anything even a hundredth as good as that.

"Wow," I said. "They'd probably love that. If that is something you'd really enjoy doing, I think you'd also score some major points with your parents."

"I like to cook. I already cook whole meals for my friends' families. They love it. I could do that with my parents and it would make it way better."

"Great! Do we need to work out anything else with that rule?"

"No. That'll actually be kind of fun."

"Fantastic. All right, on to the final contestant: no smoking pot."

"Dude, that's not even a choice. It's not like I want to smoke as much as I used to, just here and there. It's harmless. I'm not gonna stop, that's not even a choice for me."

"You know what? It actually is a choice. You may decide you don't want to stop smoking, and that's fine if you decide that, but it is a choice that you make. So I just want to support you in making the choice that best fits all your own goals for yourself. I have no attachment to whether you stop or not. Does that make sense?"

"Yeah."

"Great. So I wonder if it's worth it to you to stop for the final year so you can stay with your parents, finish High School, and get into college? That's something you'll decide – a choice that you make. So what is it about smoking pot that's so important to you?"

"It's just what I do with my friends. It's the way we hang out and chill, and have a good time."

"If you decided to stop smoking for a year so you could get the other things you want, are these the kind of friends that would support you in your choice?"

"Oh yeah, they'd be totally chill with that."

"OK, well that's great to have friends that will support you in what you choose for yourself. Do you think there are other things you could do with your friends that would be just as fun as smoking?"

"I don't know. We're not the kind of stoners that just sit around doing nothing. We do other things, they're just that much more fun when you're high."

We were approaching the airport, so I knew our conversation would have to wrap up soon. "Well, this may be something that you continue to think about. I just hope that you keep in mind all of your goals for your life, so that you're the happiest with whatever you decide."

"Yeah, thanks. At some point my parents are gonna have to drop these rules though, and give me a chance to fuck up. Otherwise I'll never be able to prove to them that they can trust me."

"I think there's some truth to that, but I think there's something else that's much more important to building trust, and you can do it with your parents even if they never give you a chance to fuck up."

"What?"

"Communication. Being in contact with them. Taking the time to try to understand what they want when you disagree, and letting them know what you want. Because your parents will notice when you're paying attention and trying to understand them, or if you're blowing them off. If they know you're listening to them, even if you disagree, that will make a huge difference.

"Think about it. If you weren't in contact with them to begin with why would they give you a chance to screw up? If there's no communication or relationship, then there's no trust, and giving you the chance to mess up doesn't really prove anything, even if you follow all the rules. Without communication and relationship, there can be no trust. They could give you a million chances to mess up, and you could pass them all, and they still wouldn't know what was going on with you. Does that make sense?"

"Yeah, it does."

"So the good news is you can work on building that trust as soon as you get home. It's going to be hard and frustrating, and there will be times when you just don't understand your parents at all, but if you work at it you'll start to build trust that way. Then when your parents give you a chance to screw up and you don't, then it'll mean something."

We pulled into short-term parking and walked inside. While we were waiting to check his bags, I said. "So it sounds like you've got ways that most of the rules will be OK now. I think the pot is the only one left for you to think about and decide for yourself what's best."

"Yeah."

"And I think you struck on something really important, and that's how to build trust with your parents, which can only make your life better for all your goals. And the key thing to building that trust is— "

" —Communication." Robbie filled in without missing a beat, catching my eye and nodding with a thoughtful expression.

Afterword

I hope you've enjoyed the stories in this book, and received value from the tools that I found vital to thriving as a leader of teens in a chaotic environment. My experiences working in the field with these kids taught me more than I could have ever learned in a book alone, so I hope you continue to explore these tools in whatever "field" you're in, whether it be the classroom, the living room, the jail room, the street, or the great outdoors.

If you found this book helpful, enjoyable, or enriching, please tell a friend and consider leaving a review on Amazon. com so that others can hear about the benefits you got from reading "Waltzing with Wolverines."

For further resources, I welcome you to visit my website www.MarkAndreas.com and sign up for my monthly blog "Tools & Tales of Change," where you can hear inspiring stories of personal change, and learn the methods used to get there. If you are interested in receiving individual coaching, or training for your group, you can also visit www.MarkAndreas.com.

Acknowledgements

I n writing these acknowledgements, I'm both amazed and touched by all the incredible, supportive people I had the pleasure of working with during my time as a field instructor for Monarch. Without you, it would have been a very different and much more trying experience. I am deeply grateful to all of you.

In particular I want to thank Nick for being the best and most supportive boss I could imagine. I also want to thank Monarch's founder and director, Dave, for all the tools he taught me, and for making it all possible. Thanks to Monarch's fabulous therapists for everything they taught me while I sat in on the kids' therapy sessions. And of course thanks to all of my incredible co-instructors, who were there with me 100% no matter what went down. Thanks also to my parents, for being a major part of helping me debrief after each 3-week expedition, and helping me plan improvements for how I led the next one. Finally, I want to thank all the kids I got to know over the course of my time as a field instructor. I thoroughly enjoyed our time together, and you taught me more than anyone.

Index

About the Author:

 **Mark Andreas** grew up in the Rocky Mountains, led wilderness trips throughout his college years, and from 2006-2008 he worked as a counselor/trip leader for the Monarch Center for Family Healing, a wilderness therapy company. At Monarch Mark led groups of troubled youth on three-week-long backpacking expeditions throughout the western United States, facilitating both individual therapy and group process on a round-the-clock basis while also teaching wilderness skills. Since working at Monarch, Mark has been in private practice offering Personal Change Coaching to individuals around the world, meeting both in-person and over Skype to help people achieve life-goals and resolve limitations using NLP, Core Transformation, and other methods for personal transformation and development (www.markandreas.com). Mark offers custom trainings nationally, is an instructor of NLP at Red Rocks Community College, and a trainer for the NLP of the Rockies' Real World Integrated NLP Practitioner Training program. His previous book, *Sweet Fruit from the Bitter Tree: 61 stories of creative and compassionate ways out of conflict,* is a collection of true stories of creative responses to conflict, endorsed by Dan Millman and William Ury.